500 THINGS TO DO *Before* YOU KICK THE BUCKET

Donald Vaughan
Christine A. Dallman
Christine Halvorson

WEST
SIDE
PUBLISHING

Donald Vaughan has made his living with words for more than 30 years. His work has appeared in an eclectic array of publications, including *Military Officer Magazine, Nursing Spectrum, Cat Fancy, MAD* magazine, and the *Weekly World News.* Donald lives in Raleigh, North Carolina, with his wife, Nanette, and their very spoiled cat, Rhianna.

Christine A. Dallman is a freelance writer who has contributed to the devotional publication *The Quiet Hour* and is a former editor and columnist for *Sunday Digest* magazine. She is the author of *Daily Devotions for Seniors,* an inspirational resource for maturing adults, as well as coauthor of *How to Let God Help You Through Hard Times.*

Christine Halvorson is a freelance writer and is also the owner of Halvorson New Media, LLC, advising businesses on how to use "social media" tools for their corporate communications. She has authored several books with Publications International, Ltd., Rodale Publishing, and Yankee Publishing, and her work has appeared in magazines and newspapers for 25 years. She lives in Hancock, New Hampshire, with her husband, Ken Sheldon, who is also a writer.

Cover Photos: Getty Images; Shutterstock

West Side Publishing is a division of Publications International, Ltd.

Louis Weber, CEO
Publications International, Ltd.
7373 North Cicero Avenue
Lincolnwood, Illinois 60712

ISBN-13: 978-1-4127-7797-1
ISBN-10: 1-4127-7797-6

Manufactured in U.S.A.

8 7 6 5 4 3 2 1

Contents

■ ■ ■ ■

Wake Up, Sleepyhead— It's Time to Start Living!

Too often we spend our days dreaming instead of doing. "If only I had the time," we say, "I'd do this and I'd go there." Well, we have news for you: The clock is ticking. You can make plans now to do great things, or you can let life pass you by.

500 Things to Do Before You Kick the Bucket is your invaluable guide to the fun, the fantastic, and the life-affirming. It contains suggested activities that cost a lot ("Stay in a five-star hotel," "Fly first class") and nothing at all ("Create a signature dish," "Write a song"). In between you'll find ideas that take you around the world ("Visit the Taj Mahal," "See the tulips in Holland"), and show you the fun that can be had in your own backyard ("Build a tree house," "Sit on your roof").

The eclectic activities recommended within this book cover a variety of categories, including personal improvement ("Get in shape"); acts of mercy ("Build a house with Habitat for Humanity"); entertainment ("Attend a laser show at a planetarium"); sports ("Visit the Baseball Hall of Fame"); and travel, both domestic ("Ride a mule down the Grand Canyon") and international ("Visit the Parthenon in Athens"). Whether you're serious-minded ("Learn the Periodic Table of Elements") or more whimsical ("Teach a squirrel to take a peanut from your hand"), we've got you covered.

But wait, there's more! Many entries also contain a sidebar, a fun fact, or a pertinent quote. Sidebars are short articles that provide additional information about a specific topic, while fun facts are exactly that—quick pieces of entertaining info that you probably didn't know before, such as the one on the right about an amazing tip. And quotes are pithy observations from the famous and the not-so-famous, just to make you think and grin.

By the way, don't feel obligated to perform all 500 activities contained within this book (though kudos if you do!). Instead, think of them as suggestions, potential stepping stones toward a better-lived life. There almost certainly will be activities that you can't or don't want to do for your own personal reasons, and that's okay. Skip those and move on to the activities that truly excite and stimulate you.

It's our hope that *500 Things to Do Before You Kick the Bucket* will stir your imagination and inspire you to create your own unique list—and act upon it. After all, life is short. And no one is going to live it for you.

❑ 1. Learn to snow ski.

Every winter, hundreds of thousands of skiers take to the slopes from coast to coast. If you don't know how to snow ski, now would be a great time to learn. After all, you don't want to miss out on the fun. Opportunities to ski are plentiful throughout the United States and abroad (unless you live in Florida, your state probably has at least one), and the vast majority of ski lodges offer lessons for beginners. Today it's the bunny slope, tomorrow you're racing down a black diamond trail!

There are two types of downhill skiing: telemark, which uses a special kind of ski, and alpine, which is more traditional. If the idea of zooming down a snow-covered hill doesn't appeal to you, there's always cross-country skiing, which is generally less difficult. Whichever you choose, you'll be able to enjoy the great outdoors while getting a terrific physical workout.

Ancient Travel on Snow

Snow skiing as winter transportation is more than 7,000 years old. It was first practiced in prehistoric Scandinavia. Carvings dating back to circa 5000 B.C. show a skier with one pole. And archeologists discovered a primitive ski in a peat bog in Hoting, Sweden, that dates back to between 2500 and 4500 B.C.

❑ 2. Learn to water ski.

Snow skiing demands an affinity for cold weather. If you're more of a warm-weather person, learn to water ski instead. This popular sport can be enjoyed on any large body of water, and opportunities are plentiful nationwide. In fact, if your region has a large public lake, chances are pretty good that someone there is renting skis and can point you toward an instructor who can get you started.

Check the Internet or your local Yellow Pages to find water skiing locations in your area.

■ ■ ■ ■

"Ocean: A body of water occupying
about two-thirds of a world made
for man—who has no gills."

—Ambrose Bierce

■ ■ ■ ■

❑ 3. Go heli-skiing.

If you're an avid skier, it's time to take skiing to the next level by going heli-skiing! In this increasingly popular sport, a helicopter transports you to a snowy area, usually high on a mountain, and drops you off so you can ski down. It's an invigorating activity that allows you to ski normally inaccessible terrain without the rigors of having to climb there.

This isn't like skiing the bunny slope, of course; heli-skiing is only for the experienced skier. But once you do it, you'll find it the experience of a lifetime. Heli-skiing excursions are available worldwide, including Alaska, Canada, New Zealand, Nepal, and Sweden. Consult your travel agent.

FUN FACT

In the western United States, mountain snow contributes up to 75 percent of all year-round surface water supplies.

❏ 4. Go tubing down a lazy river.

The sun may be hot, but the water's cool. So beat the heat by choosing a slow and safe stretch of river, putting on your swimsuit, sunblock, hat, and shades, and plunking yourself down in the river on an inner tube.

Water Safety Tips

1. Know/scout the river in advance.
2. Check river conditions with local authorities or on government Web sites.
3. Follow any posted information.
4. Only go tubing in groups, and stay together on the water.
5. Refrain from impairing your judgment or physical abilities with alcohol or drugs while on the water.
6. Wear life vests.

❏ 5. Go kayaking.

Now before you turn the page as you mumble to yourself, "No way! I'm not going to attempt the 'Eskimo roll' in a tiny boat on an icy river!" consider that there are kayaking alternatives to the extreme sport of river or whitewater kayaking, which of course, has received more exposure than its more docile cousin, sea kayaking. Sea kayaking, on the other hand, has a spectrum of possibilities, none of which requires an "Eskimo roll." One of these possibilities is recreational kayaking, which includes longer and wider (more stable) vessels than the river kayaks. Getting out on lakes and other tranquil bodies of water in recreational kayaks has grown in popularity in recent years and is a great way to get exercise while viewing the beauty of a coastline in relative quietude.

Where to begin:

- Familiarize yourself with some basics about recreational kayaking by doing some online reading and talking with experienced recreational kayakers.

- Consider taking an introductory class on recreational kayaking, one that includes actually getting out on the water.

- Rent a kayak before buying one; try out different types.

- Follow all related safety precautions, including wearing a PFD (personal floatation device) and only kayaking with a buddy, preferably an experienced person.

❏ *6. Paddle a canoe.*

If you've never paddled a canoe over a still lake, you're missing one of life's most rewarding experiences. Paddling is easier than you'd think, once you've mastered the "J-stroke"—giving a counterclockwise twist to the oar at the end of the stroke to improve efficiency and steering.

■ ■ ■ ■

"Voyager upon life's sea,
to yourself be true,
and whatever your lot may be,
paddle your own canoe."

—Sarah Bolton, "Paddle Your Own Canoe"

■ ■ ■ ■

❑ 7. Ride in a glass-bottom boat.

How would you like to explore the watery depths without getting wet? It's easy and fun when you're riding in a glass-bottom boat!

There are plenty of opportunities to enjoy this novel mode of transportation. In Florida, for example, you can book glass-bottom boat tours in both Key West and Silver Springs, near Ocala. Excursions are also available at the Aquarena Center at Texas State University in San Marcos and in Lake Superior off Munising Bay, Michigan, among others.

FUN FACT

Rod Taylor and Doris Day co-starred in the 1966 romantic comedy *The Glass Bottom Boat*, directed by Frank Tashlin.

Glass-bottom boat rides can also be found at many international resorts, especially in the Caribbean, where the water is crystal clear.

❑ 8. Take a helicopter ride.

FUN FACT

Leonardo Da Vinci sketched a primitive helicopter in 1490.

Traveling by plane is simply mundane. For a truly unique experience, take a helicopter ride! Viewing the world from a helicopter can be awe-inspiring. And there are many opportunities to do so throughout the United States and abroad. In fact, helicopter tours are available over Niagara Falls, the Grand Canyon, scenic Hawaii, Las Vegas, New York City, and many other locations.

To find out if helicopter rides are available in your area, simply type in your region plus "helicopter tours" into your favorite Internet search engine. The adventure will be worth every penny.

❑ 9. Take a hot air balloon ride.

Balloons are much more than party decorations. On a much larger scale, they can take you and your sweetie on a trip that's out of this world.

Companies that offer hot air balloon excursions can be found throughout the United States, and they're not as expensive as you might think. Rides last about an hour, but you should plan to spend three to four hours for the entire experience. Most commercial balloon excursions take place in the early morning and early evening because that's when the wind is the most calm.

The "hot air" in hot air ballooning is generated by a propane gas burner. The balloon, known as an envelope, fills with the heated air and is carried aloft. To bring the balloon safely back down, the air in the envelope is allowed to cool so that the balloon becomes gradually heavier. In between, the balloon travels wherever the wind takes it.

To find companies that offer hot air balloon rides in your area, visit www.hotairballooning.com.

Rozier and Arlandes

The hot air balloon is the oldest flight technology known to man. The first successful manned balloon flight was made in Paris by Jean-François Pilâtre de Rozier and Francois Laurent d'Arlandes on November 21, 1783.

❏ 10. Ride a gyrocopter.

Gyrocopters, also known as autogyros, are small one- or two-seater rotorcraft that raise the experience of flight to a truly visceral level. Make plans to take one for a spin—if you've got the nerve.

Gyrocopters are often sold as personal aircraft, sometimes as home-built kits. Because of their diminutive size and the skill necessary to fly one well, companies that offer actual gyrocopter rides aren't as common as other types of air excursions. They can be found, however, though more commonly outside of the United States. South Africa–based Sky Adventures, for example, offers gyrocopter and other types of air rides to fearless tourists. For info, visit www.skyadventures.co.za.

> **FUN FACT**
>
> A gyrocopter called "Little Nellie," piloted by Ken Wallis, was featured in the James Bond flick *You Only Live Twice*.

❏ 11. Ride in a blimp.

Lighter-than-air craft have been around for decades, and it's every kid's dream to see the world from their unique vantage point. If you've never taken a blimp ride, there's no time like now. There are several commercial blimps, the most famous of which belongs to Goodyear, which hovers its craft above sporting events on a regular basis. Unfortunately, the Goodyear blimp is not available to civilians, so hitching a ride with them is unlikely.

To make your dream come true, however, you can travel to northern California, where Airship Ventures offers scenic tours aboard its 246-foot, ultra-safe, helium-filled zeppelin, Eureka, which cruises at an altitude of 1,200 feet and travels 35–40 miles per hour. Depending on where you fly from, you can get a bird's-eye view of the Golden Gate Bridge, Coit Tower, the Oakland Bay Bridge, and much more. It's a trip unlike anything you've ever experienced, and one you'll surely remember forever.

The company flies from three locations: Moffett Field in Mountain View, Oakland Airport's North Field, and Monterey Peninsula Airport. The Eureka holds a dozen passengers plus crew. Tickets start at $495 for an hour-long trip, and group rates are available. For flight and ticket information, visit www.airshipventures.com.

The First Hot-Air Balloons

For centuries people have enjoyed playing with balloons and longed to take flight. It's not surprising that someone would combine the two. In fact, two brothers, Jacques and Joseph Montgolfier, invented the first known hot-air balloon in 1783. Later that year, another Frenchman, Jean de Rozier, was the first to make a balloon flight.

❑ 12. Fly in a jet fighter.

If you've dreamed of flying a jet fighter ever since you saw the film *Top Gun,* stop dreaming and start doing. Several companies offer the opportunity to climb into the cockpit of a real fighter and chase the clouds.

Jet fighter flights are available around the world, with Russia being one of the most popular. Of course, going supersonic isn't cheap, but imagine the thrill of finally satisfying your need for speed!

■ ■ ■ ■

"When once you have tasted flight you will always walk the earth with your eyes turned skyward: for there you have been and there you will always be."

—Henry Van Dyk

■ ■ ■ ■

❑ *13. Go skydiving.*

Admittedly, this activity isn't for everyone, especially those who suffer from a fear of heights. But if you're looking for extreme thrills thousands of feet above the earth, skydiving is the way to go.

There are two ways to approach this endeavor. The

The Da Vinci Parachute

The parachute is not a modern invention—Leonardo Da Vinci, the original Renaissance man, sketched the first known parachute around 1483. Unlike today's parachutes, Da Vinci's invention consisted of sealed linen held open by a pyramid of wooden poles. A parachute loosely based on Da Vinci's original design was successfully tested in June 2000.

easiest, and perhaps safest, is to go on a tandem dive, in which you are firmly secured to an experienced instructor, who does all the hard work, including releasing the chute; all you have to do scream your lungs out while you enjoy the view.

But if you're more of a do-it-yourself kind of person, you'll need to undergo training before you proceed to a solo free fall. Training options include tandem training, static line training, and accelerated free fall training. Skydiving is a sport enjoyed throughout the United States, and companies that offer both training and skydiving opportunities can be found in almost all regions.

❏ *14. Go parasailing.*

Ever have a dream in which you could fly? Make that dream a reality by parasailing. In this incredibly fun sport, you are attached to a parachute-like canopy, called a parasail, which in turn is attached to a boat by a long tow rope. As the boat picks up speed, the parasail takes you aloft. (Note: this activity is not advised for people with a fear of heights.)

Parasailing is a relatively new sport that dates back to the 1960s, but it has become very popular in recent years, especially in tourist spots with ocean access. Another version, called terrestrial parasailing, involves being towed behind a moving vehicle.

> ### Suggested Height Limits
> Altitude is everything when it comes to parasailing, but too much height can be dangerous. The suggested optimum altitude for bays and small lakes is 300 feet, and 800 feet for large lakes and the open ocean.

Enthusiasts like parasailing because it enables them to become airborne in relative safety. You can enjoy a remarkable view of the surrounding area while the wind whips through your hair, then be brought in for a gentle landing. As a result, parasailing is an activity that can be enjoyed by the entire family.

❑ 15. Go hang gliding.

Hang gliding is the closest you'll ever come to flying like a bird. It's an invigorating activity, and something everyone with a daring heart will want to try.

The sport involves the use of a glider made of a light metal frame and a fabric wing. The pilot hangs beneath the wing and controls its flight by shifting his or her body weight. Hang gliding opportunities are plentiful throughout the United States, especially in areas with hills and strong wind drafts, which are required for flight. It is a relatively safe sport, but there is always an element of danger. For further information, including the names of instructors in your state, visit the United States Hang Gliding and Paragliding Web site at www.ushpa.aero.

> ### Eilmer, the Glider
> One of the first successful hang gliders in Europe was a monk named Eilmer of Malmesbury. In 1010, he constructed a primitive hang glider and flew it from a high tower, gliding about 200 meters before landing and breaking both legs.

Hang gliding has grown tremendously in recent years, but it's not a new activity. Some of the first hang gliders—essentially manned kites—are believed to have been flown in China around the fourth century A.D.

❑ 16. Ride a zip line.

Riding a zip line—a pulley attached to an inclined cable—can be the thrill of a lifetime. Never turn down an opportunity to give it a try.

Zip lines are both a wild ride and a great way to see the scenery. Many international resorts offer zip line excursions that take you through the canopy of a rain forest or over other natural attractions. Check the Internet for zip line opportunities at your next vacation destination.

☐ 17. Go bungee jumping.

Admittedly, jumping off a tower with only an elastic cord to prevent you from going splat isn't everyone's idea of a good time. But if you're an adrenaline junkie looking for an exciting new fix, bungee jumping is the sport to try.

Though it looks dangerous, bungee jumping is actually quite safe. Most commercial bungee companies use state-of-the-art elastic cords, plus a body harness for extra safety, so your chances of getting injured are extremely slim. That said, individuals with back problems, heart problems, or any other ailment that could be exacerbated by plunging hundreds of feet while attached only to a giant rubber band should avoid bungee jumping.

FUN FACT

Bungee jumping was first documented on Pentecost Island in Vanuatu, where young men tested their courage and manhood by leaping from tall wooden platforms with vines tied to their ankles.

Bungee jumping opportunities can be found throughout the United States and across the world. Participants dive from a variety of locations, including stationary platforms, hot air balloons, or very tall structures such as bridges. One innovative company even offers the chance to jump into the mouth of a live volcano from the skids of a hovering helicopter.

❑ *18. Jump off the high dive.*

Are you a risk-taker? Show the world you've got what it takes by jumping off the high dive the next time you're enjoying a day at the municipal pool. Yell like Tarzan, and try not to do a belly flop. That would hurt.

FUN FACT

Johnny Weissmuller, who played Tarzan in 12 motion pictures, was one of the best swimmers of his era, winning five Olympic gold medals and one bronze.

❑ *19. Ride cross-country on a bicycle.*

One of the best ways to see the United States is by bicycle. If cycling cross-country has been your dream since high school, now is the perfect time to make it come true. Cycling from one end of America to the other is an intimate way to explore our nation's natural wonders and get to know its people. Along the way, you may also learn something about yourself.

A cross-country bike trip isn't for everyone, of course. It requires a commitment of at least three months—and longer if you want to stop and see the sights along the way. It also requires a certain degree of physical fitness. But if you decide to pursue this quest, you'll find it well worth your time.

Don't skimp on your bicycle—purchase the best touring bike you can afford. A top-notch repair kit is also a necessity, just in case you break down away from civilization. You'll also need sufficient money, a cell phone, and basic necessities, including toiletries and a few changes of clothes. Once you're on the road, set a comfortable pace and stick to it. You'll probably feel a little sore your first few days, but the discomfort should subside quickly.

> **Cycling Tips**
>
> If you decide to cycle cross-country, be prepared for dramatic changes in climate and terrain. Bring good-quality rain gear, cold-weather clothes, extra shoes, and sunscreen. Lastly, don't forget the maps.

❏ 20. Ride a bicycle built for two.

Yeah, it looks corny. But a bicycle built for two can be a lot of fun and a great way to enjoy a sunny day with someone you love. So suck it up and start pedaling; you won't regret it.

> **FUN FACT**
>
> HAL, the malicious computer in Stanley Kubrick's *2001: A Space Odyssey*, sings "Daisy Bell," also known as "Bicycle Built for Two," as it's being disconnected.

❏ 21. Ride a moped, and maybe buy one.

One hundred miles on a gallon of gas? That's really cool. Plus you don't need special training, and they're easy to park. So why not rent one and try it out? Afterward, consider taking the plunge by buying one. Gas prices aren't going to get lower.

> **Need a Special License?**
> Most likely not. Nevertheless, check with your state's Department of Motor Vehicles.

❑ 22. Ride a motorcycle.

A car will get you where you want to go, but there's nothing quite like riding a motorcycle. Rent one for a day and revel in the sun on your back and the wind in your face. It's an invigorating experience.

> **Cycle Inventors**
> The very first "motorcycle" was a bicycle with a coal-powered steam engine, invented by Sylvester Roper in 1867. The first gas-engine motorcycle as we know it today was built by German inventor Gottlieb Daimler in 1885.

❑ 23. Ride one of the world's fastest roller coasters.

Among thrill ride enthusiasts, speed is king. And there's no roller coaster faster than Kingda Ka at Six Flags Great Adventure in Jackson, New Jersey, which clocks in at a heart-stopping 128 miles per hour! But that's not all. Kingda Ka also holds the world record for Highest Roller Coaster with a dizzying 456 feet at its tallest point, and Largest Drop—a stomach-churning 418-foot plunge.

If you like thrill rides in quantity, visit Cedar Point Amusement Park in Sandusky, Ohio. Boasting 17 roller coasters, it's an adrenaline junkie's dream.

❑ 24. Ride a mechanical bull.

Essential Film Prop

A mechanical bull is the centerpiece of the movie *Urban Cowboy* (1980), starring John Travolta and Debra Winger. The film was loosely based on an *Esquire Magazine* profile of Gilley's Bar, written by journalist Aaron Latham.

If you've never ridden a mechanical bull, it's time to take the bucking bronco by the horns and show the world just what you're made of. Try not to cry when you get thrown off, which you almost certainly will.

❑ 25. Travel by train.

Don't be in such a rush. The next time you have to go somewhere, travel by train and enjoy the ride. Planes are great if you have to be somewhere in a hurry, but a leisurely train ride offers a wonderful opportunity to see the country in comfort.

Amtrak provides train service throughout North America. Among its more popular routes:

- The Auto Train links Washington, D.C., with Orlando. It's a marvelous way to travel to Florida without driving your car.

- The California Zephyr connects Chicago to the West and carries passengers through the Rocky Mountains for one of the most scenic train rides you'll ever experience.

- The Coast Starlight travels between Los Angeles and Seattle and features floor-to-ceiling windows in its popular Sightseer Lounge.

- The Crescent takes passengers from New York to New Orleans. Trips are offered daily.

- The Ethan Allen Express, from New York to Vermont, is the perfect way to see New England's gorgeous fall foliage.

- The Adirondack, which runs from New York to Montreal, is a nice way to travel from the United States to Canada.

- The Southwest Chief passes through the wondrous land-scapes of Arizona and New Mexico.

FUN FACT

In 1830, the steam engine "Tom Thumb" pulled the first passenger car 13 miles from Baltimore to Ellicott's Mill, Maryland.

Travel by rail has never been more fun and affordable. For schedules and other information, visit www.amtrak.com.

❑ *26. Attend a train show.*

Did you have a model train set as a kid? You weren't alone; model trains have been popular toys for generations. If it's been a while since you've enjoyed this special hobby, get off your caboose and attend a model train show.

Though model trains aren't nearly as popular among kids today as they were in years past, devotees remain passionate and enjoy sharing their love of trains with others. Numerous train shows are held across the country, and there's a good chance at least one can be found in your hometown.

For info on the next show nearest you, visit www.trainfinder.com.

■ ■ ■ ■

"I never travel without my diary. One should always have something sensational to read in the train."

—Oscar Wilde

■ ■ ■ ■

❑ 27. Stay in a five-star luxury hotel.

Vacationers often try to reduce their expenses by staying in inexpensive hotels, motels, or inns. This year, get out of your annual vacation

FUN FACT

The AAA and their affiliated bodies use diamonds instead of stars to express hotel and restaurant ratings levels.

rut by spending at least one night in a five-star luxury hotel. Sure, it'll be pricey, but there's no sin in splurging now and then. In fact, if you know in advance that you'll be staying in a five-star hotel during your trip, you'll be able to save up a little extra beforehand so that your wallet won't feel the pinch quite as badly.

To find a luxury five-star hotel where you'll be vacationing, visit www.fivestaralliance.com.

❑ 28. Ride in a limousine.

Travel in a limousine at least once. Want to go all out? Take a ride in a 1941 Cadillac Limo or a 1950 Rolls Royce.

> ### FUN FACT
> The Midnight Rider, based in California, is the world's largest limousine. It contains three lounges, large-screen televisions, and a bathroom.

❑ 29. Fly first class.

One of the greatest luxuries in life is flying first class, so the next time you travel, find out how much an upgrade will cost—then go for it. After all, you only live once.

■ ■ ■

**"Angels can fly because they
take themselves lightly."**
—G. K. Chesterton

■ ■ ■ ■

❑ 30. Smoke a Cuban cigar.

If you're going to smoke, do it in style by puffing on a pricey Cuban cigar. True Cuban-made stogies are technically illegal in the United States, but they are relatively easy to obtain elsewhere. So go across the border and enjoy yourself.

■ ■ ■ ■

"A woman is an occasional pleasure but a cigar is always a smoke."

—Groucho Marx

■ ■ ■ ■

❑ *31. Buy a really nice hat.*

People don't wear nice hats the way they used to. Throw away that ugly trucker's cap, and replace it with a more stylish and contemporary chapeau. Try on a variety of different styles before you choose; not all heads can wear all hats.

The Panama Hat

Contrary to its name, the Panama hat did not originate in Panama. It's actually a product of Ecuador, where it is traditionally woven from the leaves of the toquilla straw plant. The Panama hat saw a rise in popularity after President Theodore Roosevelt added it to his wardrobe.

❑ *32. Create a signature dish.*

You don't have to be an Iron Chef to create a delicious signature dish. All you need is a little "kitchen imagination" and some time to experiment. And if you're one of those people who's more comfortable in the garage than in the kitchen, it might be helpful to read a book on basic cooking techniques before you begin, just so you'll know the essentials. From there, it's all up to you.

There are numerous ways to create a signature dish, but one of the easiest is to take a basic meal, such as pasta, and infuse it with innovative ingredients and flavors. Instead of sautéing meat and vegetables in traditional olive oil, substitute more flavorful sesame oil. Or mix and match different spices for extra zest.

> ### Roman Delight
> The ancient Romans were adventurous eaters, and their meals often featured unusual delicacies. One popular dish was baked dormice stuffed with minced meat and spices.

It also helps to work with foods you're familiar with. For example, if you're a grill person, improve your burgers and steaks by creating your own special barbecue sauce or marinade. If baking is more your thing, strive to create a new cookie or cupcake.

❏ 33. Own a piece of jewelry from Tiffany's.

Tiffany & Co. is one of the world's most famous high-end jewelry stores. Show a bit of class by jazzing up your wardrobe with a nice Tiffany piece. Cost: Several hundred to tens of thousands of dollars. (Class doesn't come cheap.)

■ ■ ■ ■

"I never worry about diets. The only carrots that interest me are the number of carats in a diamond."

—Mae West

■ ■ ■ ■

34. Treat yourself and your significant other to dinner at a really expensive restaurant.

What's the most fancy place you've ever eaten? If all you can think of is a place with a plastic menu, then it might be time for you to treat yourself. To find the right restaurant, ask friends for recommendations—word of mouth is always the best endorsement.

■ ■ ■ ■

"Dining is and always was a great artistic opportunity."

—Frank Lloyd Wright

■ ■ ■ ■

35. Make potato chips.

Homemade potato chips are a delicious treat and easy to make. The next time you have company over, surprise them with chips à la you!

Here's how you do it:

Crum's Chips

In 1853, George Crum invented the potato chip. He worked as a chef at a hotel in Saratoga Springs, New York. After he fried thinly sliced potatoes as a variation on the traditional french fry, his snack became an instant hit.

1. Thinly slice two or three raw potatoes with a mandolin slicer.

2. Add peanut oil to a skillet or deep fryer. Heat to 350 degrees F.
3. Slowly add the potato slices; cook until crispy.
4. Place the chips on a cookie sheet covered with paper towels. Dab to remove excess oil.
5. Place chips in a large bowl and add a few dashes of salt or other seasoning. Cover and shake lightly to coat.

❑ *36. Try caviar.*

Caviar is often considered a delicacy only for the rich and famous. If you've never tried it, now's the time to live like the wealthy. Caviar is most often processed from sturgeon (black caviar) and salmon (red caviar).

"Wit ought to be a glorious treat like caviar; never spread it about like marmalade."

—Noel Coward

❑ *37. Enter a pie-eating contest.*

If you ever have the opportunity to enter a pie-eating contest, do it—especially if it's for charity. You never know when you'll get permission again to make a big pig of yourself in public.

"God always has another custard pie up his sleeve."

—Lynn Redgrave

❏ 38. Make bread from scratch.

And we don't mean with a bread machine! Bread made by hand and eaten hot out of the oven is a dying art form. Experience this joy and save money. Flour, water, yeast, sugar, salt, oil/butter, and eggs are all essentials for bread making.

"Bread is the warmest, kindest of words. Write it always with a capital letter, like your own name."

—Anonymous

❏ 39. Eat Rocky Mountain oysters.

"Rocky Mountain oysters" is a euphemism for bull testicles, a dish available at many restaurants in the western states. Try them— if you dare.

FUN FACT

Rocky Mountain oysters are also known as "prairie oysters," "mountain tendergroins," and "cowboy caviar."

❏ 40. Wade in a cranberry bog.

If your only exposure to cranberries is a dollop of cranberry sauce at Thanksgiving, get ye to a cranberry bog and have some fun! Cranberry bogs are most commonly found in the New England states. Unlike other berries, cranberries like it really wet, so your best bet is to search wetland areas.

Cranberry plants are small and scrubby, with green leaves that become tinged with a cranberry red in the autumn. The berries themselves are often submerged beneath the water, just waiting to be picked. So grab a basket and a pair of waders and dive in!

☐ 41. Roast chestnuts over an open fire.

We live in a modern age, but that doesn't mean we can't enjoy some pleasures from the past. So this holiday season, do as the song suggests and roast chestnuts over an open fire. It's a fun, as well as delicious, holiday tradition.

Never roasted chestnuts before? Here are some tips:

- Cut a small X into each nut to prevent a buildup of steam.
- Roast the chestnuts in a covered frying pan for 15–25 minutes or until they are tender.
- Serve warm with salt and cinnamon.

☐ 42. Pull taffy.

Anything worthwhile takes effort, including good candy. Instead of buying sweets at the grocery store, work up a sweat (and be hero to your kids) by pulling taffy. Recipes can be found on the Internet and in most confectioners' cookbooks.

❑ 43. Order only dessert.

The next time you dine out, exert "adult privilege" and order only dessert instead of an entrée. For dessert, have more dessert. Your family and friends may give you a frown, but deep in their hearts they will envy you. You may not want to do this around the kids.

❑ 44. Eat ice cream for breakfast.

Adulthood means being able to bend the rules now and then. Right? So tomorrow, treat yourself to a dish of ice cream or an ice cream cone, or even a sundae or milk shake, for breakfast. It may not be the most nutritious meal, but it will be fun. Don't worry—we won't tell Mom. And one time is enough.

❑ 45. Plant a garden and grow your own produce.

There was a time when almost everyone grew their own vegetables. If you have the room, consider doing the same.

Growing your own produce is fun, easy, and relatively inexpensive.

First, establish your garden space. It can be as large or as small as you wish, but it's suggested that you start small and expand as your thumb grows greener. Next, the most difficult decision you'll have to make is what vegetables to grow. Consult your local Farm Bureau Extension to find out which veggies grow best in your part of the country, as well as for gardening tips and advice.

Gardening takes time and practice to master, but it's well worth the

---

Seeds or Plants?

There are two ways to start a garden: with seeds or established plants. Seeds require more work, but they will give you more plants if germinated properly. Established plants are suggested for gardeners who have less time.

---

effort. By growing your own vegetables, you'll save money on your grocery bill and be able to give your family fresh, nutritious produce. If you grow an abundance of vegetables, you can preserve some for the off-season, give them to friends and family, or donate them to a local food bank.

Vegetable gardening is also a great way to relax and improve your health. It lets you spend time in the sun and fresh air, and working with your hands is a great way to reduce stress. For more information visit www.backyardgardener.com.

❑ 46. Share your secret recipe with a friend.

Cement the relationship you have with your best friend by sharing a secret family recipe. Every family has one, but what good does it serve to keep it to yourself? Offer your recipe, and hopefully your friend will do the same.

■ ■ ■ ■

"Friendship marks a life even more deeply than love. Love risks degenerating into obsession, friendship is never anything but sharing."

—Elie Wiesel

■ ■ ■ ■

❏ 47. Write an unexpected letter to a friend.

Technology has taken over our lives. It has invaded our homes and workplaces and has pulled us apart as a society in many ways. Take a step back to a kinder, gentler age by writing an unexpected letter to a friend—not an e-mail, but an actual letter, using a pen and paper. This is how people used to communicate, and it still has tremendous value. Use the opportunity to tell the person how much his or her friendship means to you and of all the good things he or she has brought to your life. If you have one, include a meaningful photograph of the two of you.

Electronic Communications
E-mail has become the predominant way in which human beings communicate, primarily because it's fast, convenient, and inexpensive. The volume of e-mail sent daily might startle you. According to the Radicati Group, an estimated 210 billion e-mails are sent worldwide each day.

❑ 48. Send a poem to someone you care about.

The next time you're in an eloquent mood, send a poem that expresses your feelings to someone you care about. Write one yourself or borrow the words of others; it doesn't matter as long as the words express what's in your heart. Limericks don't count.

■ ■ ■ ■

"Poetry is a deal of joy and pain and wonder, with a dash of the dictionary."

—Kahlil Gibran

■ ■ ■ ■

❑ 49. Start a new family tradition.

Tradition is an important part of being a family. Some families have numerous traditions dating back generations, while others have only one or two. This year, start a new one.

Most traditions revolve around a particular event, such as birthdays or a specific holiday. Make your new one something fun that the entire family can participate in regardless of age. For example:

- Create a special meal that's specifically for birthdays.
- Watch *It's a Wonderful Life* or some other appropriate movie on Christmas Eve.
- Celebrate the Fourth of July together at the same location.

Remember: A tradition isn't a tradition unless you do it every year.

∎ ∎ ∎ ∎

"Tradition simply means that we need to end what began well and continue what is worth continuing."

—Jose Bergamin

∎ ∎ ∎ ∎

❏ 50. *Treat your family to summer in January.*

Winter can be a months-long drag. Liven up everyone's spirits by celebrating summer in January! Have a picnic on the living room floor, complete with basket, blanket, sandwiches, and beverages. Complete the illusion by scattering rubber ants on the floor.

∎ ∎ ∎ ∎

"People don't notice whether it's winter or summer when they're happy."

—Anton Chekhov

∎ ∎ ∎ ∎

❏ 51. *Create a family tree.*

Have you lost track of your family beyond your grandparents? Many people do, which is a shame because family is our heritage and legacy. Get to know your family's path by researching your ancestors and creating your family tree. Of course, your quest will require a bit of detective work.

Start by interviewing every surviving family member you can find. Get the names of their parents, grandparents, and siblings, as well as any information they may have about other family members. Hopefully, the information you desire will cascade backward, giving you a nice family tree that covers many generations.

There will come a time, however, when you'll run out of living relatives and the path of your family tree will become unclear. There are a variety of organizations on the Internet that can research your lineage, but much of this can be done by you simply by searching public records, old newspapers, and so on. The information is there, but you'll have to work a little harder to find it.

❑ 52. Visit a relative you've never met.

We all have relatives we've heard about but never met—aunts, uncles, and cousins in far-flung places around the world. Many times, our only communication with these individuals is an annual holiday card. That's why you should get to know these long-lost relatives by paying them a visit during your next vacation.

Family is at the heart of what makes us special, and that includes distant relatives. They're an integral part of our history and heritage, and it would be a shame not to know them on a more personal level. They have stories to tell and life lessons to pass along. But some day they'll no longer be with us, so strive to make this trip sooner rather than later.

Of course, you should never arrive unannounced. It might seem like fun to surprise them by simply showing up on their doorstep, but that would be rude and potentially embarrassing. (What if they're not home?) So call first, or at least write. Unless you've been on the news lately for all the wrong reasons, they'll almost certainly be happy to hear from you.

"You don't choose your family. They are God's gift to you, as you are to them."
—Desmond Tutu

❑ *53. Write down your family history.*

Preserve your heritage by writing down your family history, stories, and favorite recipes for future generations. This is something too few families do. When older family members pass away, they often take important memories with them, leaving younger generations without them. Don't let that happen to you. Write to every living family member you can find and ask them to contribute to your special project. Request a chronology of family history, their favorite memories, and anything else they care to offer. Make copies for all involved.

"When you look at your life, the greatest happinesses are family happinesses."
—Joyce Brothers

❑ 54. Ask friends to join you in trying a new ethnic food at least once a month.

Good friends and good food . . . what could be better? Explore the food of the ethnic restaurants where you live. Or if you prefer, you can research recipes online and prepare culinary delights of the world in the comfort of your home.

❑ 55. Give one of your treasures to a younger person.

The bond between young and old can be very precious. Help establish that special connection by giving one of your personal treasures, such as a watch or ring, to a younger person, with an explanation of why it means so much to you.

❑ 56. Find someone to whom you can teach a skill.

If you've mastered a particular skill, find someone to whom you can teach it. You'll be doing them a favor by passing along your special talent. Once they have it down, ask them to pay it forward.

We All Have Skills

The skill you teach doesn't have to be complex. It can be something as simple as changing a car tire, using a piece of machinery, or fly fishing. Most importantly, make sure you and your student have fun.

❑ 57. Give a toast at a wedding.

Most people attend numerous weddings over the course of their lives, and you should toast a happy couple at least once. When you do, focus on what's special about the bride and groom, as well as what's unique about their happy union. Make the toast personal, and don't try to play the comedian. The focus of the event should be the wedding couple, not you.

Write down your toast, which should last no longer than 30 seconds, and practice it in front of a mirror. Don't try to wing it.

> **FUN FACT**
>
> There are appropriate quotes for wedding toasts on the Internet. For examples, visit http://www.freeweddingtoasts.net/.

❑ 58. Give a eulogy at a funeral.

Funerals are by nature somber affairs, but they serve an important function: to honor the deceased. As such, everyone should give a eulogy at a funeral at least once. When it's your turn, talk with friends and family of the deceased, and incorporate their thoughts and memories. A touch of humor is okay, but don't let your eulogy turn into a roast.

As with any important speech, rehearse your eulogy before you present it. And don't be embarrassed if you become tearful at the podium; it's only natural.

❑ 59. Attend a stranger's funeral.

It's been said that the death of any person diminishes us all. Show your respect for humankind by attending the funeral of a stranger and honoring that person with flowers or a donation. The highest respect would be to attend the funeral of a soldier who died in combat.

■ ■ ■ ■

> **"A man who lives fully is prepared to die at any time."**
> —Mark Twain

■ ■ ■ ■

❑ 60. Find your best friend from grammar school.

Remember the awe and wonder you felt in grammar school? It's probably been a while since you've thought about that period in your life—or the best friend who went through it with you. Now would be a great time to find that person and become reacquainted. It's easier than you might think. First, see if your friend is still living in your hometown by visiting www.whitepages.com. If he or she isn't listed, try the various social networking sites such as Facebook.com, Myspace.com, and Classmates.com. And don't forget to contact mutual acquaintances. They may know the whereabouts of the friend you're seeking.

■ ■ ■ ■

> **"What is a friend? A single soul dwelling in two bodies."**
> —Aristotle

❑ 61. Tell your life story to a stranger.

Everyone has a fascinating tale to tell, and though you may not believe it, you do as well. So just for the fun of it, sit on a park bench and regale a stranger with your life story à la Forrest Gump.

❑ 62. Return to your childhood home and ask for a tour.

The next time you return to your hometown, drop by your childhood home and ask for a brief tour.

Home is where the heart is, and the many wonderful memories you collected in the house where you grew up helped make you who you are today. Explain to the new owners why you would like to see the house one last time, and share a few fun anecdotes from your childhood. Don't stay too long, though. And make sure you thank your hosts for their time and consideration when you leave.

■ ■ ■ ■

"The things which the child loves remain in the domain of the heart until old age."

—Kahlil Gibran

■ ■ ■ ■

❑ 63. Buy your favorite childhood story.

Everyone has a favorite storybook from childhood. If you've lost yours, buy another copy and read it; you'll find that even in adulthood it's a treasure to be cherished. And if you have children of your own, share the experience with them.

■ ■ ■ ■

> "While thought exists, words are
> alive and literature becomes an escape,
> not from, but into living."
>
> —Cyril Connolly

■ ■ ■ ■

❏ 64. Watch reruns of a television show you loved as a kid.

Relive beloved childhood memories by watching reruns of your favorite television show from when you were a kid. Between DVDs and channels such as TV Land, almost every pro-

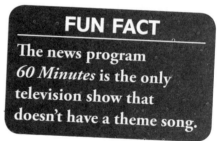

FUN FACT

The news program *60 Minutes* is the only television show that doesn't have a theme song.

gram from your youth is available. Invite your own children to join you.

❏ 65. Climb a tree.

The next time you're stressed or life is getting you down, climb a tree. There's just something about sitting on a high branch watching the world go by that makes you realize your problems aren't as bad as you think they are.

Trees are very beneficial. In addition to providing shade on hot summer days, they...

- Absorb carbon dioxide and produce oxygen.
- Reduce noise pollution by acting as sound barriers.
- Stabilize the soil and prevent erosion.
- Improve water quality by filtering rain water and protecting aquifers and watersheds.

❑ 66. Ride on a tire or tree swing.

Need a break from the rigors of adulthood? Then ride a tire swing or a tree swing. Both will have you feeling like a kid again as you push yourself higher and higher. Reflect on the good old days.

■ ■ ■ ■

**"If you carry your childhood with you,
you never become older."**

—Tom Stoppard

■ ■ ■ ■

❑ 67. Build a tree house.

You don't have to be a kid to build a tree house. Just think of it as an opportunity to create that special outdoor getaway you've always wanted. Any kind of tree will work, as long as it's large and strong enough to support the structure you want to build. Design it first, then buy the necessary materials. Depending on how big you want

FUN FACT

Some municipalities require a permit for the construction of a tree house, so make sure you check before driving your first nail.

to go, your tree house can include furniture, windows, and even electricity. Listen to your inner child for ideas, and have fun.

❑ 68. Twirl a hula hoop.

Twirl a hula hoop around your waist for at least five minutes without the hoop dropping or your touching it with your hands. It's not as easy as you think.

FUN FACT

The word *hula* in hula hoop comes from hula dancing in Hawaii.

❑ 69. Play hopscotch without missing a beat.

Be a kid again and play hopscotch. You can do it with kids, friends, or by yourself. But whatever you do, have fun!

FUN FACT

The Roman army invented hopscotch as a way to train its soldiers to improve their footwork.

Draw lines in the dirt of a play area, or better yet, use white or colored chalk to draw a design on pavement. You can use the typical design with ten squares or be creative. And use a favorite charm that won't break to toss into the squares. Do it until you go through it without missing.

❑ 70. Attend your class reunion.

Has the fact that you were a geek in high school prevented you from attending your class reunion? Don't let it. Class reunions are a wonderful opportunity to get reacquainted with old friends and make new ones.

Time is a great equalizer, and the more years that pass, the more everyone from high school has in common, including growing families, interesting jobs, and fascinating life experiences. So the next time you receive an invitation to your class reunion, say yes—and wear your teenage geekiness as a badge of honor, comfortable in the knowledge that you've done well in life and have much to be proud of.

❑ 71. Make contact with a high school classmate you haven't seen since graduation.

The Internet has opened up communication in mind-boggling ways. Online sites such as Classmates.com are linking up old high-school classmates in ways you could never have imagined before the age of computers and the Internet. Add to this MySpace, Facebook, Friendster, and other such online "personal page" sites, and there's almost no one you can't find by poking around in cyberspace for a couple of hours. If you have an old friend from high school in mind already, start with Classmates.com. Get the ball rolling and see what happens. Good luck!

■ ■ ■ ■

"You can make more friends . . . by becoming interested in other people than you can . . . by trying to get other people interested in you."

—Dale Carnegie

■ ■ ■ ■

❑ 72. Make a realistic New Year's resolution.

Next New Year's Eve, make a realistic resolution—one you can actually keep—and write it on the first day of every month in your calendar. You'll be more likely to stick to it if you're reminded regularly. Celebrate when you've accomplished your goal.

■ ■ ■ ■

"Be always at war with your vices,
at peace with your neighbors, and let each
new year find you a better man."
—Benjamin Franklin

■ ■ ■ ■

❑ 73. Write a personal mission statement.

Every successful corporation has a mission statement. To enhance your own success, write a personal mission statement with rules to live your life by. Place it where you'll see it every day, and work hard to live up to its ideals.

■ ■ ■ ■

"Success is not the key to happiness.
Happiness is the key to success. If you love what
you are doing, you will be successful."
—Albert Schweitzer

■ ■ ■ ■

❑ 74. Organize your photos.

If you're the designated family shutterbug, plan a weekend to organize your photographs. Arrange them by date, event, and location, and make sure everyone is identified on the back of each. That way, your family can enjoy them for generations to come.

■ ■ ■ ■

"Sometimes I do get to places just when God's ready to have somebody click the shutter."

—Ansel Adams

■ ■ ■ ■

❑ 75. Make and bury a time capsule.

You never know what tomorrow will bring. As a special gift, build and bury a time capsule so that your grandchildren will know a little bit more about you and the era in which you lived.

First, create a container out of a long-lasting material such as plastic or PVC. Avoid wood, which can rot, or metal, which can rust. Your goal is to build a capsule that will remain impenetrable for as long as it is buried. Next, select the items to be included in the time capsule. These might include a daily newspaper (preserved in a plastic sleeve); photographs that illustrate your

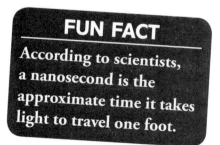

FUN FACT

According to scientists, a nanosecond is the approximate time it takes light to travel one foot.

life and times; a CD or DVD with words, images, or music; a popular toy; and so on. Your selections should be unique to you but also offer a glimpse into the world as it was when you put the time capsule together.

Once your capsule has been sealed, find a suitable place on your property to bury it, and write down its exact location. Put this information in a safe place, such as a safe deposit box or even in your will. Make sure other family members are aware of the capsule and when you would like it to be unearthed and opened.

❏ 76. Investigate your dream trip.

A dream untended is a dream unrealized. Ask your travel agent how much a trip to your dream destination would cost by every mode of transportation. Then make it happen.

> **FUN FACT**
> Approximately 2.8 million hotel rooms are sold per night in the United States. That's enough for every person in Dallas, Detroit, and Denver combined.

Most people travel by plane, but depending on what your dream destination is, it might be cheaper to drive or travel by bus or train. Be up-front with your travel agent regarding how much money you have to spend. He or she will be happy to work with you.

❏ 77. Take a vacation by yourself.

If you have never taken a major trip by yourself, you really should—and we're not talking about a business trip in which you have clients to see or a conference to attend.

Take a trip entirely of your own making and purpose. Fellow travelers and locals are more likely to engage you when you're alone. They will help you find your way, will chat with you on an airplane, and will offer sightseeing insights. It's also freeing to set your own agenda, to decide by yourself whether it will be sushi or ribs for dinner, and to go with the flow of your own whims.

> **"I, who travel most often for my pleasure, do not direct myself so badly."**
> —Michel de Montaigne

❏ *78. Get in shape.*

If you're an average American, you can probably stand to lose a few pounds. Enough with the excuses—do it now! Unless you're morbidly obese (defined as being 20 percent or more over your ideal body weight), getting into better shape isn't as difficult as it might appear. All you need is confidence, dedication, and willpower.

Your first inclination may be to try one of those crazy diets you see advertised on television. Don't do it! According to the American Dietetic

---

The Consequences of Being Fat

Obesity affects much more than just your appearance—it can also influence your self-esteem and your quality of life. Worse, being overweight carries very serious health risks, including heart disease, diabetes, stroke, and depression.

Association, the majority of diets simply don't work. And even if you do succeed in shedding a few pounds, chances are good that you'll only regain them later.

There are two simple concepts to successful weight loss: eat fewer calories and exercise more. Here are a few helpful tips:

- Processed foods are full of empty calories. Whenever possible, substitute fresh fruits and vegetables.

- Reduce your fat intake by eating lean whenever possible.

- Drink plenty of water. Avoid soft drinks.

- Ask a friend to work out with you. Companionship makes exercising easier.

- Walking is the best exercise you can do. It's safe, easy, and free.

- Set a realistic target weight, and work toward it in increments.

- Consult your doctor before beginning any diet or exercise regimen.

❑ *79. Face your greatest fear.*

Everyone has something they're afraid of, something that prevents them from achieving their full potential. This year, make a vow to face your greatest fear—and defeat it.

The first thing you must do is acknowledge and define your fear. It could be anything: a fear of failure, a fear of the unknown, a fear of taking risks, or a fear of losing something dear to you. Visualize your fear and determine exactly how it is adversely affecting your life.

Overcoming a fear that is holding you back depends on what it is and how deeply it is ingrained. For some people, conquering a fear may be as simple as writing it down and making a determined effort not to let it impact their lives. But for others, the fear may be so deep that it requires the help of a therapist or counselor. If that's you, don't hesitate to get the assistance you need.

❑ 80. Look at a strand of your hair under a microscope.

When it comes to our bodies, most of us tend to focus on the big picture, while ignoring what we can't easily see. Use a microscope to marvel at a strand of your hair. You'll be amazed at what you observe.

Human Hair

Because human beings are mammals, hair covers our entire bodies except for the soles of our feet, the palms of our hands, and our lips. Pigment gives our hair color. When we age, our hair receives less pigment, which is why it turns white or gray.

❑ 81. Get an education.

Knowledge is the key to success, so make education a life-long endeavor. If you didn't graduate from high school, it's not too late to get your General Educational Development (GED) certificate. If you didn't go to college, enroll in night school or get your degree online. If you're a college graduate, take courses through your local continuing education program.

You can also help educate others by teaching a subject of interest through your local adult education program. It's a great way to give back to your community, and most adult ed programs don't require a teaching degree.

❑ 82. Take a night class just for fun.

Education should be lifelong, so take a college night course just for the fun of it. In addition to boosting your knowledge, you might also make some new friends.

■ ■ ■ ■

"I have never let my schooling interfere with my education."

—Mark Twain

■ ■ ■ ■

❑ 83. Attend a high school play.

It may not be the best drama you've ever seen, but it will be some of the best time and money you've ever invested. You could even be seeing one of the next big Hollywood stars.

Even if the performance is rough in spots or downright awful all the way through, it's not just a play you're watching on stage. It's far more than that. You're witnessing the development of young men and women as they take risks many of us would never dare take; you're looking on as they sound the depths of their abilities and dreams. It's part of the metamorphosis of young life into adulthood, and you are helping it by showing your support, by being there as the curtain goes up.

■ ■ ■ ■

"A dramatic critic is a man who leaves no turn unstoned."

—George Bernard Shaw

■ ■ ■ ■

❏ 84. Watch Native American tribal dancers perform.

Native American tribal dances are amazing to behold, and they include initiation dances, worship dances, and ceremonial dances. Some are performed by individuals, others in groups. Many involve elaborate clothing and headdresses.

There are many opportunities to view tribal dances performed just as they were hundreds of years ago. Some cultures offer regular performances for tourists on their homelands, while others can be seen at special

FUN FACT

The first people to come to North America were from Asia about 20,000 years ago.

events around the country. Consult the Internet to see if Native Americans routinely perform in your area or will be part of an upcoming festival or other event.

☐ 85. *Sit on your roof and watch the world.*

When the weather is fine, the roof of your house is a great place to watch the world go by. Your neighbors may think you're silly, but who cares? Go for it! (Just be careful.)

■ ■ ■ ■

"There are worse things in life than having fun."

—Bill Harris

■ ■ ■ ■

☐ 86. *Memorize the "Who's on First?" routine.*

For baseball fans, the three funniest words in the English language are "Who's on first?" It's Bud Abbott and Lou Costello's most famous comedy routine, and it continues to amuse. Entertain your friends by memorizing the entire dialogue. You'll find it at www.baseball-almanac.com/humor4.shtml.

FUN FACT

Abbott and Costello first performed "Who's On First?" on *The Kate Smith Hour* radio program in March 1938.

❏ 87. *Introduce someone to your favorite book.*

Hello, _____. I'd like you to meet my favorite book, _____. You can certainly think of a less...silly introduction; nevertheless, tell someone about a book that has had a significant impact on you. What better suggestion can you give to a trusted friend or a recent acquaintance?

■ ■ ■ ■

"The reading of all good books is indeed like a conversation with the noblest men of past centuries who were the authors of them."

—René Descartes

■ ■ ■ ■

❏ 88. *See the circus.*

Give your inner child some new memories by attending the circus the next time it comes to

FUN FACT

American showman P. T. Barnum was the first owner of a circus to trans-port his circus by train.

town. And don't forget the cotton candy. It's an even better experience if you take children with you.

❏ 89. *Attend a* Star Wars *convention.*

Few movie franchises have experienced the continued popularity and cultural impact of the *Star Wars* saga. If you're a fan of the Force—and even if you aren't—attend a *Star Wars* convention the next chance you get. You'll never look at the movies the same way again.

Star Wars conventions are held throughout the United States and abroad on a regular basis. Fans gather to discuss the movies, meet the stars and special effects creators, and revel in all things *Star Wars*. It's just like a *Star Trek* convention, only with fewer pointy ears.

Consult the Internet for the next *Star Wars* convention near you.

Lucas's Inspirations

Star Wars (1977) was George Lucas's first movie after *American Graffiti* (1973). He spent two years fine-tuning the script. When not at his typewriter, Lucas read comic books and watched old Buck Rogers serials for inspiration.

❑ 90. Attend an ice-skating entertainment show.

The next time Stars on Ice, Holiday on Ice, or another ice-skating entertainment show comes to your town, book a ticket to see Olympic champions or a show that features some of your favorite Disney characters. You'll be glad you did.

FUN FACT

The Ice Capades toured for more than 50 years, beginning in 1940, but went out of business more than a decade ago. Since then, attempts to revive it have failed.

❑ 91. Attend a laser light show at a planetarium.

If you're lucky enough to live near a planetarium that offers a laser light show, don't pass up the opportunity to enjoy this unique mind-bending experience. The lights will dazzle you.

FUN FACT

The music of most laser light shows revolves around a particular rock band. One of the most popular is Pink Floyd.

❑ 92. Enter a video game competition.

Today's generation of cyber athletes have no interest in running faster or jumping higher. Instead, they're cybergeeks who tromp opponents in high-stakes video game competitions. If you have outstanding skills in a particular game, it's time you stepped up and played with the big boys.

In recent years, video game competitions have become extremely popular and can be found in most major cities. Some of the larger national competitions draw hundreds of contestants, with impressive prize money and prestige going to the winners. To find out about competitions in your town, contact your local game shop or check the Internet.

FUN FACT

According to a study by the Pew Research Center, more than half of American adults age 18 and older play video games.

❑ 93. Host a '60s party.

If you're in the mood for a really fun theme party, think no further than the 1960s! A '60s party is very easy to pull off. Simply have your guests dress up in '60s-era garb (hippie, go-go dancer, rock musician), and decorate your house in a '60s motif (bead curtains, black light, Che Guevara poster, large throw pillows, incense, lava lamps).

Of course, a '60s party is a bust without the right music. Best bets: The Beatles, Rolling Stones, The Doors, and Jimi Hendrix.

FUN FACT

A total of 32 musicians and bands performed over four days at Woodstock in 1969. Richie Havens opened the festival, and Jimi Hendrix closed it.

❑ 94. Host a '70s party.

FUN FACT

The movie *Saturday Night Fever* was based on a 1976 *New York Magazine* article titled "Tribal Rites of the New Saturday Night" by Nik Cohn.

If you're too young to remember the '60s, host a '70s party instead! Guests should dress in appropriate attire (think leisure suits and miniskirts), and your home should be decorated in '70s chic, right down to the de rigueur Farrah Fawcett poster.

As for music, you can't go wrong with disco, the clarion call of the "Me Decade." Best bets include The Bee Gees, KC and the Sunshine Band, and Donna Summer. Conclude the evening with "Disco Inferno" by The Trammps.

❏ 95. Meet your favorite celebrity.

Would you like to meet your favorite celebrity? It's easier than you might think. Celebrities frequently appear at events and venues that put them in contact with fans. For example, if your favorite star is appearing in a play in your hometown, attend the play and ask for a meet-and-greet or wait at the stage entrance out back; most stars take a few minutes after each show to sign autographs. You can also meet celebrities at charity events, autograph shows, and at their favorite hangouts.

When you approach your favorite celebrity, be polite and respectful of his or her time. Stars are people, too. (It also helps if your favorite celebrity is known for being a friendly person.)

■ ■ ■ ■

"The image is one thing and the human being is another. . . . It's very hard to live up to an image."

—Elvis Presley

■ ■ ■ ■

❏ 96. Be a celebrity for a day.

Just because you're not globally famous doesn't mean you can't act like it. For one day, pretend to be a celebrity.

Turn your friends and family into rabid paparazzi, taking your picture, videotaping your every move, and bombarding you with personal questions as you try to go about your daily business. Enlist others to be your bodyguards and entourage or diehard fans begging for your autograph, which you should refuse. Meanwhile, demand to be left alone while unabashedly posing for the cameras.

La Dolce...Camera?

The word *paparazzi* is derived from a character named Paparazzo in the film *La Dolce Vita*, directed by Federico Fellini. The director said the character, a photographer, reminded him of "a buzzing insect, hovering, darting, stinging."

❏ 97. Be on television.

You don't have to be famous to be on the boob tube. In fact, if reality television has taught us anything, it's that fame is generally the result of being on TV, not the other way around.

One of the best reasons to be on television is the opportunity to call all of your friends and nonchalantly ask, "Did you catch me on TV last night?" Luckily, there are a variety of ways to make this happen. One of the easiest is to be in the right place at the right time, such as in the grocery store when the local TV news crew shows up to interview shoppers. You can also volunteer to be in a television commercial, say, for a local car dealer. Sure, there's no money in it, but who cares—you're on television!

❏ 98. Try out for a reality TV show.

Eager for your 15 minutes of fame? Try out for a reality TV show! There are essentially two types of reality programming—scripted continuity shows such as *The Hills* and participatory shows such as *The Amazing Race*, *Wife Swap*, *Big Brother*, and *Survivor*.

Obviously, the latter shows are your best bet. Most continually solicit potential participants through the network's Web site and require you to submit a lengthy application form and often a videotape of yourself. Not surprisingly, thousands of people apply each season, so your chances of being selected are relatively slim.

Many reality shows also accept applicants via agents. This may sound as though it eliminates the "reality" aspect, but keep in mind that reality programming is still show business. With that in mind, you may want to approach a local casting agent about auditioning for your favorite reality show.

Reality Warnings!

Being on a reality TV show may sound like fun, but there can be consequences. You may be asked to perform strenuous or uncomfortable tasks or engage in behavior that goes against your nature or beliefs. And you have little say in how you will be portrayed—it's all up to the producers, per the contract you will be required to sign.

❑ 99. Sing at a karaoke bar.

Release your inner Elvis by singing your heart out at a local karaoke bar. And don't worry about being a bit out of tune—you won't be the only one.

FUN FACT

The word *karaoke* means "empty orchestra" in Japanese.

❏ 100. Dress up for Fantasy Fest.

Every October, more than 100,000 revelers fill Key West, Florida, for Fantasy Fest, one of the largest public costume parties in the United States. Put on your gaudiest outfit (or just paint your body like many do) and pay a visit—you'll have a ton of fun.

> **FUN FACT**
>
> Like Mardi Gras (and for many of the same reasons), Fantasy Fest is definitely an adult event.

❏ 101. Play cowboy or cowgirl.

It's the advice of singer Willie Nelson that mammas shouldn't let their babies grow up to be cowboys. If your mom is the only reason you're selling insurance instead of riding the range, it's not too late to do something about it. Several working cattle ranches offer opportunities for amateur cowpokes to saddle up and enjoy the real-life cowboy experience. For example, at the Hunewill Guest Ranch in Bridgeport, California, just east of Yosemite National Park, guests are encouraged to help gather and sort some of the more than 1,000 cattle that must be herded into corrals for vaccinating or branding. Those with advanced horsemanship skills can also learn how to rope cattle and assist with more serious activities.

Several ranches in Colorado, New Mexico, and elsewhere offer similar opportunities for paying guests. Depending on where you stay, you can participate in such traditional cowboy chores as driving cattle, mending fences, and branding calves. Playing cowboy can be tiring work, and it doesn't come cheap. But you'll return home with a previously unknown sense of accomplishment. Talk with your travel agent or consult the Internet for more dude ranch information.

■ ■ ■ ■

"A cowboy is a man with guts and a horse."

—William James

■ ■ ■ ■

❑ *102. Invent something.*

Are you chock full of great ideas? Improve the lives of others by inventing something useful.

There are two ways to approach this project:

1. Invent something unique.

2. Improve on something that already exists.

Sketch a detailed design of your invention, then build a prototype to make sure it actually works. If it does, take the next step and look into getting a patent for your product. For information and advice, visit the United States Patent and Trademark Office at www.uspto.gov.

Edison's Successes and Flops

Thomas Edison received an astonishing 1,093 patents over his lifetime and gave the world the phonograph, the lightbulb, and the motion picture camera. Edison, however, also had a few failures, including sound movies and a more practical way to mine iron ore.

❏ 103. Start a collection.

Almost everyone has a special passion, something that brings them joy. Figure out what yours is, then start collecting it. From fine art to old comic books, what you collect doesn't matter as long as the thrill of the hunt makes you happy.

■ ■ ■ ■

"It is perhaps a more fortunate destiny to have a taste for collecting shells than to be born a millionaire."

—Robert Louis Stevenson

■ ■ ■ ■

❏ 104. Make up your own secret language.

The next time you have a few hours to kill, create your own secret language. (Pig Latin doesn't count.) Once it is perfected, teach it to someone you love. Then your deepest secrets will be known only to each other.

Twin Language

Some twins have developed their own unique form of communication in childhood, a phenomenon known as *idioglossia* or *cryptophasia*. The development of an actual secret language between twins, however, is quite rare and usually occurs only in instances of extreme isolation.

❑ 105. Make a snow angel.

Fresh fallen snow is pretty to look at, but it's even more fun to play in. The next time you experience a substantial snowfall, act like a kid and make a snow angel. Better yet, grab the family and fill your yard with angels.

■ ■ ■ ■

"A lot of people like snow. I find it to be an unnecessary freezing of water."

—Carl Reiner

■ ■ ■ ■

❑ 106. Build a giant sand castle on the beach.

The next time you're at the beach, play Frank Lloyd Wright and build a giant sand castle, complete with moat and turrets. Try not to cry when the ocean washes it away.

FUN FACT

Plastic forks, knives, and spoons make castle-building easier.

❑ 107. Paint a picture good enough to hang on your wall.

While da Vincis and Picassos only come around every few hundred years, there's no reason you can't set up an easel, don a beret, and try brushing paint on a canvas. If you weren't born with natural artistic talent, take a class and then paint something good enough to hang on your wall. What you paint doesn't matter if it comes from your heart.

■ ■ ■ ■

"Every artist dips his brush in his own soul, and paints his own nature into his pictures."

—Henry Ward Beecher

■ ■ ■ ■

❑ *108. Build a model airplane or ship.*

One sure way to stay young is to hold on to the joys of childhood. Bring back fond memories of your early years by building a model airplane or ship. If you're a parent or grandparent of young children, invite them to join the fun.

> **FUN FACT**
>
> The earliest model kits were made of balsa. Today, the majority are manufactured using injection molded polystyrene plastic.

❑ *109. Build a dollhouse from scratch.*

You can buy a dollhouse or put together a dollhouse from an assembled kit with plastic pieces, but it is far more rewarding when you build a wood dollhouse from

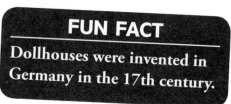

> **FUN FACT**
>
> Dollhouses were invented in Germany in the 17th century.

scratch and then paint it yourself. It may take you hundreds of hours, but the person you give it to will treasure it for a lifetime.

❏ *110. Build a piece of furniture.*

There's tremendous satisfaction that comes with working with your hands. If you're halfway decent with a saw and hammer, craft a piece of quality furniture that you can hand down to your children and your children's children.

It doesn't have to be anything complex. Tables, bookcases, and stools are all relatively easy to construct using a few pieces of good-quality wood and basic tools. If you're a skilled woodworker who's eager for a challenge, however, consider building something a bit more fancy, such as a desk or a chest of drawers.

Books with easy-to-follow plans for building furniture can be found in most hardware stores.

Tools You'll Need

The key to good furniture-making is using the right tools. At the minimum, you'll need a ruler or tape measure, hammer, handsaw, chisels, plane, power drill/screwdriver, router, braces, and table saw.

❏ *111. Make a log sculpture with a chainsaw.*

Chainsaws aren't usually associated with fine art, and yet a growing number of people are using them and other power tools to create amazing works of art with logs. With a little practice (okay, a lot of practice), you can, too.

Find a large log, secure it with sandbags or clamp it so it won't shift, and rough out a design in chalk or a permanent marker. First, use your freshly sharpened chainsaw to carve the image, and then use your smaller power tools to tailor the details. Any kind of wood can be used, but make sure you treat it once you're done. If you've never used a chainsaw before, take a basic use-and-safety course before you sculpt.

❑ *112. Dig for fossils.*

If you're like most people, you're probably fascinated with prehistoric creatures. So try something different for your next vacation by digging for fossils.

The eons-old remains of dinosaurs and other critters lie waiting to be discovered throughout the United States. In fact, depending on where you live, there could be a treasure trove of fossils buried in your backyard. Some states, such as Utah and Montana, are renowned for the amount and diversity of well-preserved fossils they contain. To find out about fossil-digging opportunities in your area, consult your local geological, archaeological, and historical societies. They can make you aware of the best sites for public digging and offer tips on what you are likely to find.

Once you've located a favorable site, you'll need some equipment. At the very least, bring a mason's hammer, shovel, pick, brushes, and a sifting pan or box. Be aware that not all fossils are large, so carefully examine the material you dig up. A real treasure might be no larger than your thumbnail.

From Bones to Fossils

Fossilization occurs when an animal is buried rapidly in a soft sediment such as sand, mud, or ash. As the animal's soft tissue decays, the remaining bones and teeth lodge in with the soil, which hardens into rock. The fossils later become exposed through erosion.

❑ 113. Look at the moon through a telescope.

Thrill seekers, look up! Viewing the moon through a telescope (or even a good pair of binoculars) is a kick! That bright orb you've always admired from a distance becomes even more spectacular upon closer inspection. On a clear night, moon mountain ranges, barren lava plains, and deep craters are visible even at moderate magnification levels. Astronomers advise looking at the

Those Moon Craters Have Names!

Galileo was among the first to look at the moon through the lens of a telescope and see its beauty and complexity up close. Then in 1651, Giovanni Riccioli introduced a system for naming the craters of the moon. The largest craters have been named after famous astronomers or other people of historical significance. Today, the International Astronomical Union (IAU) controls the naming of lunar features.

moon while it is in phase, rather than when it is full, since it's the shadows that allow the viewer to see details on the surface. (A full moon, they say, is blinding and not much can be seen because of the bright rays.)

❑ *114. Go spelunking.*

Spelunking is a fancy word for exploring caves—an activity everyone should experience sometime in their lives. A wide variety of cave exploration opportunities can be found throughout the United States, and many companies offer spelunking excursions. (Check the Internet for caving organizations in your state.)

> ### Do's and Don'ts in Spelunking
>
> Caving can be dangerous and unpredictable, so never go alone. In addition, always make sure someone knows where you're going and when you will return, and never enter a cave passage unless you're certain you can make it out safely.

Caving can be fun and exciting, but it's much more rigorous than visiting larger, more famous caves, most of which have walkways for visitors. Depending on the cave you're exploring, you may have to lower yourself down with ropes and crawl through tight passages, so it's definitely not an activity for someone who suffers from claustrophobia.

❑ *115. Pan for gold.*

Need a little extra money? Pick Mother Nature's pocket by panning for gold!

Begin by choosing a state known for gold deposits, such as Alaska, California, Georgia, or Montana. A natural-resources expert should be able to point you toward promising locations. Once you've locate a good spot, you'll need a pan, a mesh box for separation, and something to hold the gold flakes you find. Since you'll be working near water, waders are probably a good idea, too.

For the government's take on panning for gold, visit http://pubs.usgs.gov/gip/prospect2/prospectgip.html.

❑ 116. Mine for rubies.

Rubies are gorgeous gems, and they look radiant in jewelry. But why buy them when you can mine them yourself? North Carolina and Tennessee are home to several companies that offer the opportunity to try your luck. Mining for rubies is great family fun, and you get to keep all the gems you find. Many sites also contain emeralds and other valuable stones. Keep in mind that the gems you find will need to be polished for their real beauty to burst forth.

❑ 117. Hike a glacier.

Ages-old and integral to carving the planet's features, glaciers are one of nature's most fascinating phenomena. For the trip of a lifetime, plan a glacier-hiking vacation. Hiking excursions are available to glaciers around the world, including Matanuska Glacier in Alaska. If you'd rather go international, consider a trip to New Zealand, where hiking at Fax and Franz Joseph Glaciers has become a very popular tourist

On the Move

Glaciers are known for their slow advance, but not all glaciers move at a glacial pace. Surging glaciers can travel 10 to even 100 times faster than more traditional glaciers.

activity. Glaciers can also be found in such faraway places as Venezuela, Pakistan, Switzerland, Greenland, and Austria.

Remember: Glaciers tend to be cold, so dress accordingly. And be a good guest by making sure you leave nothing behind.

❑ *118. Explore the ocean.*

You don't have to be Jacques Cousteau to explore inner space—that is, the world's oceans. The wonders of the sea can be yours by going snorkeling, scuba diving, or submerging in a submarine.

Snorkeling and scuba diving are extremely popular activities worldwide and relatively easy to enjoy. Snorkeling is the easiest and least costly, but you're restricted in what you can see because you're limited to the water's surface.

For those who really want to experience the ocean's majestic beauty, scuba

Do It by Submarine

A novel way to explore the ocean is via submarine. True submarines are rarely available to civilians, but regions with a large reef, such as the Great Barrier Reef in Australia, often offer excursions on a special craft known as a semi submarine that brings you face-to-face with the ocean's denizens without fully submerging. Many tourist resorts offer similar opportunities.

diving is a better option. You'll need to take a diving course and buy or rent your equipment, but you'll be able to explore a much deeper and more expansive area. Best of all, dive excursions are available almost everywhere that water touches a beach.

❏ 119. Climb the tallest mountain in your state.

Life is all about reaching for the sky, and one simple way to do that is to climb the highest mountain in your state. For some people, this accomplishment will be fairly easy. The highest peak in Florida, for example, is Britton Hill in Walton County—barely a knoll at just 345 feet. Others, however, have quite a challenge ahead of them, especially those living in Alaska (Mount McKinley is 20,320 feet), California (Mount Whitney is 14,494 feet), and Washington (Mount Rainier is 14,410 feet).

If the highest peak in your state is more than a molehill, you should not attempt this feat without adequate training. This means being both physically fit and experienced in mountain climbing. If you're new to this activity, join a local mountaineering club, many of which have regular expeditions to their state's highest points.

To find the highest peak in your state, visit http://geology.com/state-high-points.shtml.

■ ■ ■ ■

"Of all the fire mountains which
like beacons, once blazed along
the Pacific Coast,
Mount Rainier is the noblest."

—John Muir

■ ■ ■ ■

❑ 120. Write to your favorite living *author, and tell this author why you enjoy his/her work.*

The most meaningful feedback for an author doesn't come from editors or critics, but from readers themselves. Why not send an encouraging note to your favorite author? It may just be the best thing they've read in a long time!

■ ■ ■ ■

"Those who are lifting the world upward and onward are those who encourage more than criticize."

—Elizabeth Harrison

■ ■ ■ ■

❑ 121. Write an entry on Wikipedia.

Wikipedia (www.wikipedia.org) is an online encyclopedia that is written and edited by everyday Janes and Joes like you. Many contributors are experts in a particular field, but you don't have to be a world authority to participate. If you're knowledgeable about a specific subject, create an entry and share your

FUN FACT

Wikipedia is a combination of the words *wiki* (from the Hawaiian word meaning "fast") and *encyclopedia*.

knowledge with the world. The site, which currently has more than 12 million entries, is big on information citation, so be prepared to let the world know where your information comes from.

❑ 122. Tour a big newspaper printing plant.

While you can, take a tour of a plant that prints a major newspaper. The "web presses" used in this process are particularly fascinating. Admit it. You've never really thought about how those pages all stick together, have you?

❑ 123. Write a letter to a company whose product you like.

Is there a product you really like? Then write a nice note to the company president or CEO, and let him or her know specifically what it is you enjoy about that product and how long you've been buying it. If you've found a novel use for the product, let the person know that, too.

Your letter will almost certainly brighten someone's day (who doesn't like being told they're doing a great job?), and you may even receive some money-saving coupons in return.

124. Write a letter to your political representative.

Most people write only when they have something to complain about. Take the high road and write a letter to your political representative or your daily newspaper praising a person or group that is doing something good in your community.

125. Volunteer on a political campaign.

All politics aside, it needs to be noted that working on a political campaign is excellent on-the-job training, providing skills you might find useful in the future. Aside from the satisfaction you get from working for a cause or person near and dear to your heart, you'll likely be learning new skills no matter how late in life you take advantage of this opportunity. You'll also be working alongside energetic people, and some of them probably will be quite different from you. You'll get to learn the "issues" from the inside out. Maybe you'll get to plan a fundraiser or stand next to a network television news personality or the governor of your state. No matter how the campaign turns out, you'll have had an experience worth savoring.

It's easy to find a particular candidate or cause to work for these days with a simple search on the web. Then just call up the office and say you're available. No doubt they'll welcome you with open arms.

Find a candidate or a campaign you're interested in at http://www.votesmart.org.

❑ 126. Write the president of the United States, and let him know how you think he's doing.

The president may not read your note, but somebody will. Send some advice, and not just a complaint. Today there's an easy online form: http://www.whitehouse.gov/contact/.

Otherwise, put pen to paper and send to:

The White House
1600 Pennsylvania Avenue NW
Washington, D.C. 20500

■ ■ ■ ■

"This at least should be a rule through the letter-writing world: that no angry letter be posted till four-and-twenty hours will have elapsed since it was written."

—Anthony Trollope

■ ■ ■ ■

❑ 127. Shake hands with a U.S. president.

There's no greater thrill than shaking hands with a current or former president. Luckily, there are several ways you can make this happen. Being invited to the White House is perhaps the most exciting way to meet a sitting president, but that's something only a small number of Americans ever get to experience. For most people, it's easier to meet a former president at a public appearance. Book signings are ideal. Most presidents write their memoirs after leaving office, then tour the country to promote them. And some presidents write much more. Jimmy Carter, for example, is a prolific author and relatively accessible at public events.

❑ 128. Participate in a formal debate.

If arguing is one of your favorite pastimes, put your powers of persuasion to good use by participating in a formal debate. Debating is a lot of fun and can make you a more effective communicator. It's one thing to trade barbs with your friends, but it's quite another to stand up in front of a panel of judges and passionately defend a particular position.

Many cities, large colleges, and major universities have organized debate clubs. An Internet search should help you find those in your area. Stand tall, and remember: "Because I said so!" is not necessarily the best way to conclude an argument.

■ ■ ■ ■

"It is better to debate a question without settling it than to settle a question without debating it."

—Joseph Joubert

■ ■ ■ ■

❏ 129. Serve on jury duty.

If you've managed to stay out of the courtroom so far, don't even think about wiggling out of an opportunity to serve on a jury if you're summoned. With rare exceptions, it is the law for you to serve. Being part of our legal process is a unique opportunity to get a behind-the-scenes look at the institutions that keep our country running smoothly.

❏ 130. Memorize the Preamble to the Constitution.

It's a single sentence of 52 words in its entirety. If each day you commit a new phrase to memory (using the commas in the text as dividers between phrases), it would take you only eight days to memorize the entire text. Piece of cake!

Preamble to the United States Constitution

We the People of the United States, in Order to form a more perfect Union, establish Justice, insure domestic Tranquility, provide for the common defence, promote the general Welfare, and secure the Blessings of Liberty to ourselves and our Posterity, do ordain and establish this Constitution for the United States of America.

So what is the Preamble? It's a brief introductory statement outlining the fundamental purposes and concerns as well as the guiding principles that the founders had in mind as they framed the Constitution. And what would those be? In a nutshell, they include forming a strong union, establishing justice, preserving homeland peace and security, promoting the well-being of U.S. citizens, and protecting liberty, both now and in generations to come.

While you're at it, you might even choose to read the Constitution itself if you haven't ever done so. After all, it is the document that is the bedrock of the freedoms American citizens have enjoyed now for more than two centuries.

❑ 131. Complete the Sunday New York Times crossword puzzle.

If you're looking for an invigorating mental challenge, consider the Sunday *New York Times* crossword puzzle. It's one of the most difficult in the world, and it's like forcing your brain to run a marathon. Impress your friends by completing it in pen.

❑ 132. Buy a membership to your local museum.

Community support of the arts is vital to their continued growth, so buy a membership to your local museum, even if you visit just once a year. Your own cultural awareness will grow as well.

■ ■ ■

"The only time I feel alive is when I'm painting."
—Vincent Van Gogh

■ ■ ■

❑ 133. Become a docent at a local museum.

Docent is a fancy word for guide. Volunteer at your favorite museum and share your passion with others. You will expand your knowledge far beyond what you would gain as a tourist.

❑ 134. Witness a solar eclipse.

Few natural phenomena are as impressive as a solar eclipse. Because a total solar eclipse is extremely rare, the next time one occurs, do what you must to see it in person—even if it means traveling halfway around the world.

A solar eclipse results when the Moon passes between the Sun and the Earth, so that the Sun is obscured. In some solar eclipses, the Sun is only partially blocked out, while in others, it is completely covered. (In a lunar eclipse, the Earth passes between the Sun and the Moon, causing the same effect on the Moon.) Solar eclipses occur several times a year around the world, though totality occurs far less frequently. For a schedule of upcoming solar eclipses, visit www.mreclipse.com.

Visual Precaution

Gazing at the Sun during an eclipse can cause eye damage. Although it is safe to view a solar eclipse when the Moon totally blocks the Sun, it is dangerous to the eyes whenever they are exposed to the Sun, even briefly. Therefore, view an eclipse safely by using an authorized solar filter.

❑ 135. See a tornado live.

For the ultimate adrenaline rush, see a tornado—live!

While most people (wisely) run in the opposite direction when faced with an oncoming twister, a growing number of meteorological thrill seekers actually pursue them, just for fun. Several companies offer storm-chasing tours during tornado season (check the Internet). They use the latest high-tech gadgetry to study weather patterns and pinpoint the likeliest spots for tornadoes to form. There are no guarantees that you'll see a tornado up close, but it'll still be a vacation you'll remember for the rest of your life.

The Frequency of Tornadoes

The regional frequency of tornadoes depends on the season. The southeastern United States tends to be hardest hit during the spring months, while the central United States sees a higher risk from March through May. And in the summer, the shift tracks further north with the jet stream.

❑ 136. Take the Polar Bear Plunge.

Most people would never consider jumping into an icy body of water in the dead of winter. And yet, for a hearty few, it's a great way to ring in the New Year. Are you ready to take the Polar Bear Plunge?

Many major cities, including Chicago and Milwaukee, have hosted Polar Bear Plunges for years. Some even use the event as a fund-raiser for charity. So remember, your shivers are going to a good cause.

To find out if your municipality hosts a Polar Bear Plunge, contact your local Chamber of Commerce or that of the largest city on a nearby body of water.

☐ 137. Spend Christmas on the beach.

Christmas is supposed to be a joyous holiday, yet many people dread it because of the stress involved. If that sounds like you, leave your anxieties at home and spend next Christmas on a tropical beach with someone you love.

■ ■ ■ ■

"It is Christmas in the heart that puts Christmas in the air."

—W. T. Ellis

■ ■ ■ ■

☐ 138. Sleep in a haunted house or hotel.

Do you believe in ghosts? Test your personal fear factor by spending the night in a haunted house.

Since haunted houses are difficult to find (unless it's Halloween), consider a haunted

FUN FACT

The eccentric Sarah Winchester, widow of gun magnate William Wirt Winchester, spent 38 years enlarging her home, which has become known as "The Winchester Mystery House." This San Jose, California, mansion is said to be haunted and is now a popular tourist attraction.

hotel, of which there are several throughout the United States. The Anchorage Hotel in Alaska, for example, has had so many ghost sightings over the years that it keeps a special guest ghost log in which visitors can share their encounters.

Consult your favorite Internet search engine to find a haunted house or hotel in your area.

❑ 139. Turn your home into a haunted house on Halloween.

If your neighborhood contains a lot of children, treat them to something special next Halloween by turning your home into a haunted house. It'll require a little work, but the expression on their faces will be well worth it.

There are two ways to approach this endeavor: Use your house or use your yard. If you expect a lot of little visitors, turning your yard into a spooky spectacle might be the better—and safer—way to go.

■　■　■　■

"Where there is no imagination there is no horror."
—Arthur Conan Doyle

■　■　■　■

❑ 140. Spend a night in a historic hotel.

Going on vacation? Cancel your reservation at that cheap flea trap and spend the night in a historic hotel instead.

Every major city has a hotel of historic importance. To see what's available in your region, consult the National Trust Historic Hotels of America (www.historichotels.org). Its database features more than 220 hotels that have maintained their historic architecture and ambiance.

■ ■ ■ ■

"The great advantage of a hotel is that it is a refuge from home life."
—George Bernard Shaw

■ ■ ■ ■

❑ *141. Dance the hora.*

The next time you're invited to a Jewish wedding, bar mitzvah, or bat mitzvah, make sure you dance the hora, a circle dance commonly performed to the song "Hava Nagila." It's a joyous celebration!

FUN FACT
The hora is the national dance of Romania.

❑ *142. Skip in public.*

Unleash your inner kid and skip in public. Sure, you'll look goofy, but you'll also feel more alive.

■ ■ ■ ■

"I still get wildly enthusiastic about little things. . . . I play with leaves. I skip down the street and run against the wind."
—Leo Buscaglia

■ ■ ■ ■

143. Have a pillow fight.

Don't be a stuffed shirt. Tomorrow morning, start an impromptu pillow fight and include everyone in your house. Use your softest pillows. And try not to cover the place in goose feathers. Afterward, treat everyone in the battle to a nice breakfast out.

144. Fly a kite on the beach.

Remember the fun you had flying kites as a kid? Take that enjoyment to a whole new level by flying a kite on the beach.

145. Memorize the names of all of the presidents— in order.

How many presidents have there been? From George Washington (elected in 1789) to our current president, Barack Obama, the United States has had 44 presidents in all. Only 43 men, however, have been sworn into office. How can this be? Well, Grover Cleveland served two non-consecutive terms as the 22nd and 24th president.

William Henry Harrison was in office only 32 days (the shortest time in office), while Franklin D. Roosevelt was the only president to serve more than two terms (making him the longest-serving president). Four presidents have died in office of natural causes, one president resigned, and four presidents were assassinated. Do you know who they were?

❑ *146. Learn the states' nicknames.*

Everyone needs a special trick to impress people at parties. If you don't have one, learn the nicknames of all 50 states. Start with Alabama (The Yellowhammer State) and continue through Wyoming (The Cowboy State). Go to this Web site to get started: www.50states.com.

> **"Titles are but nicknames, and every nickname is a title."**
> —Thomas Paine

❑ *147. Have your caricature drawn at an amusement park.*

What a fun way to capture the memory of an enjoyable time! If you're not familiar with the art style, it's one that political cartoon satirists often use, exaggerating and distorting the essence of a person or thing, while leaving the likeness quite identifiable.

❑ 148. Have a star named after you.

If you can't be a movie star, do the next best thing and have a celestial star named after you! Several companies offer star registration services. Just check the Internet.

■ ■ ■ ■

"When it is darkest, men see the stars."

—Ralph Waldo Emerson

■ ■ ■ ■

❑ 149. Have your portrait painted.

Photographs are so modern. Go the more classic route by hiring an artist to paint your portrait. Then present it to someone special as a gift.

■ ■ ■ ■

"Who sees the human face correctly: the photographer, the mirror, or the painter?"

—Pablo Picasso

■ ■ ■ ■

❑ 150. Set a world record.

An easy way to gain fame is to set a world record. So figure out what you can do best—then go for it!

London-based Guinness World Records certifies all official world-record attempts in a wide variety of categories. You probably aren't the world's tallest man or shortest woman, so your best bet is to either establish or beat a

world record for a specific activity, such as jumping rope, singing nonstop, or walking backward.

For information on what's required to set a world record, visit www.guinnessworldrecords.com.

❑ 151. Learn the alphabet backward.

Remember the childhood thrill that came with mastering the alphabet? Enjoy the adult equivalent by learning to recite the alphabet backward. It's a feat that will amaze your friends—and particularly children.

❑ 152. Memorize your favorite quotes.

Sometimes others have expressed our thoughts far better than we could. To add a bit of spice to future discussions, memorize your favorite quotes and use them in a conversation when appropriate. Your family and friends will be impressed by your keen mind.

❑ 153. Memorize a favorite poem.

Show everyone what a cultured person you are by memorizing your favorite poem and reciting it before them. (Ribald limericks don't count.) Better yet, memorize a famous love poem and surprise your sweetie by reciting it over a romantic dinner. No doubt, you will be quite charming.

> **Poetic Tip**
> One helpful way to memorize a lengthy poem is to repeatedly write it down in long-hand.

❑ 154. Learn to speed read.

Speed reading is a skill that can benefit you in many aspects of your daily life. Become a speed reader and watch the words fly by. A good speed-reading program will help you read faster while improving comprehension and word retention. With a little practice, you'll be able to zip through *War and Peace* in an evening!

A variety of speed reading programs are available through the Internet. You're encouraged to shop around, however, because all courses are not the same, and scams do exist. For a review of available programs and recommendations of the best, visit www.thespeed readingreview .com.

> **FUN FACT**
> In 2007, Anne Jones of London read *Harry Potter and the Deathly Hallows* in 47 minutes, 1 second—an average of 4,251 words per minute!

❑ 155. Learn greetings in a variety of languages.

One can never have too many friends. Learn greetings in a variety of languages, then take a trip around the world so you can put your newfound knowledge to use. Take a fun photo of every new friend you make.

❑ 156. Learn a new language.

Research shows that learning a new language helps offset age-related losses. These days, you can find lessons in just about any language online, and often at low cost, or you can buy an inexpensive course on CD-ROM. For better socializing possibilities, however, why not enroll in a class at the nearest community college or adult-ed program? Combine the best of both worlds, and go learn a language in a country in which it is spoken. Immersing yourself in the culture and country goes a long way toward learning.

■ ■ ■ ■

"Those who know nothing of foreign languages know nothing of their own."

—Johann Wolfgang von Goethe

■ ■ ■ ■

❑ 157. Learn sign language.

It's a beautiful language! American Sign Language (ASL) is not just English put into gestures. It's something entirely different. It's a language in its own right with a grammar all its own. What many may not know is that the elements of movement within ASL do not involve only hands and fingers. Engaging the entire body is necessary to communicate. Signing uses the upper torso, arms, and head, with the face being extremely important, since facial expressions convey tone and inflection that enhance meaning. As you learn ASL, you'll also want to study its cultural context, since deaf culture is rich in its own traditions, stories, faux pas, and celebrities.

FUN FACT

Back in 1620, Spaniard Juan Pablo Bonet wrote the first well-known book of manual alphabetic signs for the deaf.

❏ *158. Learn the Periodic Table of Elements.*

How well do you know your elements? If you haven't thought about them since your high school chemistry class, challenge yourself to memorize the entire Periodic Table of Elements. You can find this table online at www.chemicalelements.com.

❏ *159. Research a topic you're passionate about at the National Archives.*

The National Archives is a national treasure, housing both mundane and important government documents. To find clues about your family's history, prove a veteran's military service, or just research a topic in history, this place has nearly everything. And if it doesn't, the staff knows who does. Maybe you want to draw your own conclusions on the JFK assassination or read the history of Yellowstone National Park. It's all there; start your search at http://www.archives.gov/research/.

❑ 160. Learn to identify the constellations.

Most people, when they gaze at the night sky, see only stars. Amaze your friends and family by connecting these celestial dots and learning a few constellations.

Grouping stars into recognizable figures dates back thousands of years and was done to assist herdsmen, farmers, sailors, and others who relied on the night sky for direction. They're a fast and an easy way to tell which direction is which.

The International Astronomical Union has defined 88 official constellations—most are based upon the ancient Greek myths. Among the recognized constellations are all 12 signs of the zodiac. A great way to learn the constellations is to visit your local planetarium.

Varying Viewpoints

The constellations are not universal. Various cultures have noted different patterns in the sky and have named them accordingly. Only a few constellations, such as Orion and Scorpius, which look very much like their names, have wide acceptance.

Books on astronomy and the many astronomy-related Web sites on the Internet can also be useful.

❑ 161. Learn to can fruit.

Canning fruit (and vegetables) is a traditional American activity, and much easier than you think. If your parent or grandparent is an old-fashioned canner, turn to them for advice. If not, visit the many Web sites, such as http://www.pickyourown.org/allaboutcanning.htm, that offer helpful tips and recipes for the home canner.

Canning is a great hobby because almost any kind of fruit or vegetable can be home-preserved. Best of all, your favorite foods will be available year round.

Appert's Fruity Concoction

Nicolas Appert of France developed one of the first methods of long-term food preservation at the invitation of Napoleon, who needed a way to keep food safe for soldiers on the move.

❑ 162. Take a cooking class.

A local restaurant, a kitchen store, an upscale market, a B & B, a community college—all of these places may offer you a chance to take a simple one-hour cooking class or an entire week of lessons. Decide your skill level and your interest level first. Even if you've been cooking for decades, you can always learn something new by watching the pros.

Cooking Vacations

Lots of places are turning cooking into a vacation destination. Search the Internet for cooking vacations, and see if there's a class in a place you've always wanted to visit. Italian in Tuscany? Gourmet in Napa Valley? Why not?

❑ 163. Take a first-aid class.

What a First-Aid Kit Should Contain

Every home should have a well-stocked first-aid kit. You can buy one at any grocery store, or make your own by stocking bandages, gauze, adhesive tape, scissors, aspirin, isopropyl, antibacterial gel, and other necessities in a well-marked box.

You never know when a medical emergency will arise, so it's important that you be prepared. If you haven't already taken a first-aid course, make an appointment to do so immediately. It could save your life or that of someone you love.

Almost every municipality offers first-aid courses through the Red Cross or a local hospital. Such courses are usually held in the evenings and may run over several classes. Take the most comprehensive course you can find.

❑ 164. Learn CPR.

Are you a lifesaver? Learn CPR, and you just might be one day. CPR stands for cardiopulmonary resuscitation. It's a technique used for reviving or keeping alive a victim of cardiac arrest, drowning (or near drowning), or other instances in which a person's breathing or heartbeat has stopped. People practiced elements of CPR as early as 1740, but it wasn't until 1960 that people began to practice CPR in the form that we are familiar with today.

It was the American Heart Association that started to train physicians

FUN FACT
CPR doubles a person's chance of survival from sudden cardiac arrest.

to use CPR. Subsequently, this training became available to the general public. Today the American Heart Association continues to orchestrate and facilitate training opportunities within communities nationwide.

❑ 165. Go to clown college.

Are you constantly getting in trouble for clowning around? Learn to do it right by going to clown college! It used to be that the only official clown college in the country was affiliated with the Ringling Brothers Circus. Today, however, there are more than a dozen independently run clown schools across the United States. Some teach traditional circus clowning, while others specialize in birthday clowning. Either way, you're going to have a great time.

For information about clown schools in your area, visit http://www.clownevents.com/list-schools.shtml.

❑ 166. Learn one or two truly impressive magic tricks.

Everyone loves a good magic trick, and learning some impressive sleight of hand is easier than you think. The key to success is practice, practice, practice. You never know when a little prestidigitation will come in handy. Magic tricks are great for breaking the ice at parties, impressing a first date, or winning a bar bet. Magic is also a fun way to improve your hand-eye coordination.

The best place to learn some nifty tricks is your local magic store. Several easy-to-master tricks are also available at www.freemagictricks4u.com.

❑ 167. Learn to throw a boomerang.

Boomerangs are typically associated with Australia, but you don't have to be from Down Under to learn how to properly throw these remarkable flying sticks. Most commercial boomerangs come with instructions on how to throw. Tips can also be found at www.boomerangs.org.

■ ■ ■ ■

"The game of life is like the game of boomerangs—deeds and words return to us sooner or later with astounding accuracy."

—Florence Skinner

■ ■ ■ ■

❑ 168. Learn ballroom dancing.

You don't have to be Fred Astaire or Ginger Rogers to dance well, but you probably will need to take lessons. Sign up. You never know when you'll be called on to do the tango.

■ ■ ■ ■

"We're fools whether we dance or not, so we might as well dance."

—Japanese proverb

■ ■ ■ ■

❑ 169. Learn to surf.

If Frankie Avalon and Annette Funicello could learn to surf, you can too! Okay, most of Frankie's and Annette's surfing was done on a soundstage, but that doesn't mean you can't learn to surf for real. The sport is popular wherever the ocean hits the beach, and most of the really popular surf spots offer instruction as well as equipment. All you have to do is ask (and pay).

Surfing requires balance, coordination, and physical fitness. Once you've mastered the basics, you'll be gliding between the waves as if you were born on a board.

■ ■ ■ ■

"Surfing soothes me, it's always been a kind of Zen experience for me."

—Actor Paul Walker

■ ■ ■ ■

❑ 170. Attend a Renaissance festival.

Hie thee thither! Grab a turkey leg and find a good seat for taking in the jousting games. Take a step back in time, and immerse yourself in the magic of a Renaissance festival, which includes a menagerie of period-costumed entertainers, music and theatrical acts, thematic arts and crafts for sale, and of course, food.

Most of these festivals seek to recreate the setting of an English village around the reign of Elizabeth I (1558–1603), a time considered representative of the heart of the Renaissance.

FUN FACT

There are more than 25 large-scale festivals scattered throughout the United States.

Shows include short (usually comedic) musical and dramatic presentations on a stage, à la Shakespeare, with doses of audience participation. Often, falconers exhibit their trained large birds of prey. Wandering performers, such as jugglers, singers, and various "characters," liven up your experience as you walk through the fairgrounds. Larger festivals host jousting tournaments with rival knights who seek victory and honor. You can try your skill at axe throwing or archery or enjoy a ride on a live animal or a human-powered swing. Plan to spend the better part of a day taking in the shows, sights, and sounds of the festival. Bring your camera: There are generally some goofy (jester-style) hats to try on—a fun photo memory.

❏ *171. Visit a sweat lodge.*

For a truly unique experience, visit a sweat lodge. Sweat lodges are a form of ceremonial sauna, which Native Americans traditionally use for important rituals. For many, participation in a sweat lodge ceremony can be very therapeutic in that it can help you find your spiritual center and improve your health.

Sweat lodges come in various designs and sizes. In most cases, rocks are heated in an outside fire and then placed in a pit in the middle of the room. Some sweat lodge ceremonies involve chanting,

What to Wear

Clothing requirements vary among sweat lodges. In same-sex environments, participants may be nude or wear just a towel, as in a traditional sauna. When visiting a sweat lodge, avoid wearing metal jewelry; it can get hot enough to burn your skin.

drumming, or wailing. Commercial sweat lodges can be found around the country. Instructions for constructing your own are available on the Internet.

❏ *172. Visit a rain forest.*

You might want to pack your umbrella for this one. Rain forests, as their name denotes, are characterized by high rainfall, anywhere from 68–78 inches annually. Though we often envision rain forests as Tarzan-inhabited jungles, there are two different types of rain forests: tropical and temperate. Tropical rain forests are found near the equa-

> **FUN FACT**
>
> Rain forests that once covered 14 percent of earth's surface have dwindled to 6 percent. Yet these critical ecosystems house more than half the world's plant and animal species.

tor between the Tropics of Cancer and Capricorn. These fit the jungle description with which we're most familiar. Temperate rain forests are in the temperate zones of North America (e.g., the Pacific Northwest and British Columbia) as well as Europe, East Asia, Australia, and New Zealand. These less typical rain forests, nonetheless, hold their own kind of mystique and beauty.

❏ *173. Visit a greenhouse or conservatory.*

Everyone needs to commune with nature once in a while. It's easy if you live in the country; less so if you live in the big city. Whatever your situation, the next opportunity you get, spend some time in a greenhouse or conservatory.

Most commercial greenhouses are open to the public, and the owners don't mind if you just want to walk through and enjoy what they have to offer. Marvel at the wide variety of plants available, and feel free to ask questions. (Of course, the kind thing to do is to buy something at the end of your visit.)

❏ 174. See a geyser.

FUN FACT

Yellowstone National Park has a webcam pointed at Old Faithful and a time indicator showing when it will "blow" next. Check it out!

Geysers are just plain cool. Travelers can find major geyser fields in Yellowstone National Park (United States), Valley of Geysers (Russia), El Tatio (Chile), Taupo Volcanic Zone (New Zealand), and throughout Iceland.

❏ 175. View a meteor shower.

We call them "shooting stars," but actually they're not stars. They're meteors—a collection of particles, generally thought to be the ice and dust remnants of comets—which are also orbiting the sun, and we see them when they collide with the earth's atmosphere.

FUN FACT

Meteor showers are named for the constellations from which the shooting stars appear to fall, a spot in the sky known as the radiant.

It's their friction with the atmosphere that causes them to heat up and glow. While meteors can be seen on any clear night (with more of them visible after midnight), your best chance for seeing them is during a meteor shower. Meteor showers occur over a period of days or weeks with a peak time for optimal viewing.

❏ 176. See a volcano.

Although you may not want to get too close, no picture can do justice to seeing a live volcano with your own eyes. Mount St. Helens still hiccups steam and ash plumes while visitors stand at observation areas a good distance away. Hawaii's live volcanoes spew red-hot lava from their cones and send it flowing down their sides, a sobering demonstration of nature's raw power. Live volcanoes can also be found in Indonesia, New Guinea, the Philippines, In-dia, Japan, Russia, New Zealand, Alaska, California, Mexico, Central America, the West Indies, the Mediterranean, Iceland, and Antarctica. Take your pick, and plan your trip.

❏ 177. Drive up Mauna Kea, the world's tallest mountain.

"But I thought Everest was the world's tallest mountain!" you may protest. Well, here's the explanation: Although the peak of Mauna Kea is 13,803 feet above mean sea level, it is 33,476 feet

FUN FACT

Mauna Kea means "White Mountain" in the native Hawaiian language, a reference to the dormant volcano's white peak during winter months.

above its base on the floor of the Pacific Ocean. By this second measure, Mauna Kea on Hawaii's Big Island can boast its world-record stature.

178. See Mount McKinley in Denali National Park in Alaska.

Mount McKinley (20,320 feet) may not be the highest mountain on Earth, but it's certainly no molehill. In fact, McKinley has a larger rise than Everest. Here's why: Although Everest is

> **FUN FACT**
>
> *Denali,* meaning "The Great One," is the Athabaskan name for Mount McKinley. In fact, the state of Alaska currently recognizes this mountain by this name.

about 9,000 feet higher (measuring from sea level), its base sits on the Tibetan Plateau, which is about 17,000 feet high. Thus the mountain's actual vertical rise is a little more than 12,000 feet. By contrast, the plateau on which the base of McKinley sits is at 2,000 feet, giving McKinley an actual rise of 18,000 feet! So if you want to climb higher, scale Everest. If you want to climb farther, McKinley's your peak.

179. Visit Glacier National Park.

If you love to hike, then this park will thrill the sock liners right off your feet. With 700 miles of trails (some of which follow old routes used by trappers in the early 1800s) winding throughout the park's astounding terrain, there's no end to the adventures you can experience in this pristine wilderness in northern Montana. Other highlights of the park include the presence of wildlife, such as white-tailed and mule deer, American elks, moose, bighorn sheep, and mountain goats, as well as grizzly and black bears, mountain lions, lynx, red foxes, coyotes, and wolves. (It's not unusual for hikers to carry "bear bells" to prevent unwanted surprise encounters with foraging bears along the trail.)

❏ *180. Visit Yosemite National Park.*

Yosemite National Park in California is one of nature's great natural wonders. From the towering heights of El Capitan and Half Dome to the tranquil meadows on the valley floor, from thundering waterfalls (including the tallest waterfall in North America) to the Merced River meandering through the valley, it is a place of unmatched beauty.

The park is open year-round, though the entry roads are often closed by snow between November and May. Summers are quite busy in the park. To plan your trip, go to www.nps.gov/yose.

■ ■ ■ ■

"It is by far the grandest of all the special temples of Nature I was ever permitted to enter."

—John Muir

■ ■ ■ ■

❑ 181. Visit Yellowstone National Park.

It's an icon! America's first national park was established in 1872 and remains a feast of nature for visitors from around the world today. The park acreage lies over territory in three Western states: Wyoming, Montana, and Idaho. It is home to wildlife most of us have only read about in books: bison, grizzly bears, wolves, elks, foxes, and other wilderness creatures. Of course, there's also Old Faithful and other geysers. (Yellowstone contains approximately one half of the world's geothermal features with more than 10,000, including more than 300 geysers scattered throughout the park).

The park also boasts its own canyon, called the Grand Canyon of the Yellowstone with tremendous waterfalls plunging down into its depths. There's a great deal of historical information available within the park too: For example, at the North Entrance, there's an arch of which the cornerstone was laid by President Theodore Roosevelt. A visit to Yellowstone is actually a "two-fer" with Grand Teton National Park just outside of Yellowstone's South Entrance.

❑ 182. Ride a mule down the Grand Canyon.

It may be good enough for some just to peer down into the Grand Canyon's grandiosity. But if you're there, why miss the chance to actually descend this awe-inspiring natural wonder, to touch its walls and feel its breath on your face? Why not clamber onto the back of a sure-footed mule and make the descent toward the Colorado River below? There *are* some reasons you might not be able to ride: (1) if you're

afraid of heights;
(2) if you weigh more
than 200 pounds;
(3) if you're less
than 4 feet, 7 inches
tall; (4) if you can't
understand English
to follow the wran-
glers' directions; or

(5) if you have any health conditions that may pose a problem. If none of these conditions disqualify you, then you're good to go!

❑ 183. Visit Mammoth Cave in Kentucky.

Mammoth Cave National Park in Kentucky features the longest known cave system in the world, with more than 360 miles explored. The next time you're in the Bluegrass State, pay it a visit.

The National Park Service offers a variety of tours ranging from one to several hours in length. Most are electrically illuminated, but two are lit only by lamps carried by visitors. Other tours take the more adventuresome paths through some of the less developed parts of the cave system.

184. Visit Mount Rushmore.

To truly appreciate this monument, read and view the interpretive information. A picture of a man working inside a nostril gives you a sense of the proportions and helps you understand just what a feat it was to carve these great faces in the mountain.

Mount Rushmore National Memorial: Frequently Asked Questions

Q: Who created the sculpture?
A: Gutzon Borglum and 400 workers

Q: How much did the sculpture cost?
A: $989,992.32

Q: How long did it take to build?
A: 14 years (1927–41)

Q: Are the faces eroding?
A: No. The estimated erosion rate is 1 inch every 10,000 years.

Q: Were there any deaths during the carving?
A: None.

(Adapted from FAQ from www.nps.gov/moru/)

---

185. See Meteor Crater in Arizona.

About 50,000 years ago, a meteor crashed into the earth and created a gigantic hole. During

FUN FACT

Meteor Crater lies at an elevation of about 5,709 feet above sea level and is about 4,000 feet in diameter and some 570 feet deep.

the past century, tens of thousands of tourists have come to peer down this impressive, hugely popular crater. If you haven't already, become one of them. Make sure to stop at the Visitor Center as well to learn the history and science behind the crater's formation.

186. Visit Carlsbad Caverns in New Mexico.

Do you like exploring caves? Well, then go to Carlsbad Caverns National Park in the Guadalupe Mountains. You won't be disappointed. It contains some of the most colorful stalactites, stalagmites, and malachite-colored pools in the world.

FUN FACT

Carlsbad Caverns has the second largest cave chamber in the world. Its "Big Room," a natural limestone chamber, is almost 4,000 feet long, 625 feet wide, and 350 feet high at the highest point. The Sarawak Chamber in Malaysia is the largest in the world.

187. Hike the Appalachian Trail.

A truly memorable way to celebrate a major milestone in your life is to hike the Appalachian National Scenic Trail—all 2,175 miles of it.

Completed in 1937, the Appalachian Trail is the nation's longest marked footpath. It extends from Georgia to Maine, touches 14 states, crosses six national parks, and traverses eight national forests along the way. (It also involves numerous state and local forests and parks.) More than 2,000 rare, threatened, endangered, and sensitive plant and animal species can be found along the Appalachian Trail, which makes it extremely popular with nature-lovers and environmentalists.

According to the Appalachian Trail Conservancy, the trail offers something for every level of hiking experience, though a beginning-to-end journey is advised only for the most skilled because some segments of the trail can be quite rigorous.

❑ 188. Hike through the Petrified Forest National Park in Arizona.

What would it be like to turn into a rock? If you're curious, then go see the Petrified Forest between Holbrook and Navajo, Arizona, where this park contains one of the world's largest and most colorful concentrations of petrified wood. There are many kinds of hiking opportunities, from short walks to much longer trails.

❑ 189. Ride a bike on the Virginia Creeper Trail.

It's been said that the best things in life are free, and that includes the Virginia Creeper Trail, a 35-mile stretch of natural Virginia beauty that's a favorite among cyclists and hikers. If you've never visited this part of the Old Dominion State, you're in for a real treat.

The Virginia Creeper Trail stretches from Abingdon to Whitetop, near the North Carolina border. It passes through some of the most scenic areas of backcountry Virginia, and is rich in regional history. The trail gets its name from the "Virginia Creeper," which is the nickname that the locals gave to the train that traveled from Abingdon to Damascus, and later to Elkland, North Carolina, in the early 1900s. The train was named after the tenacious native vine that grew beside its tracks.

❑ 190. Visit Niagara Falls.

Niagara Falls is perhaps the most famous waterfall in North America, an attraction that draws millions of tourists from around the world each year. It's one thing to see it on television or in a movie, but the sheer power of the falls is something that can be truly appreciated only in person.

Niagara Falls can be enjoyed from both the American side and the Canadian side. On the American side, the falls can be viewed from walkways along Prospect Point Park, which also features an observation tower and the dock for the popular Maid of the Mist tour boat. In addition, the falls can be seen from Goat Island, which is accessible by automobile.

One of the highlights of the Canadian side is Queen Victoria Park, which boasts gorgeous gardens and observation platforms from which visitors can view both the American and Horseshoe Falls. There are also underground walkways that take visitors into observation rooms that make it feel as if you are actually in the falling waters. While visiting the Canadian side, you should also go to the top of Skylon Tower, which provides the best overhead view of the falls. You can also see Toronto in the other direction.

❏ *191. Stand under a waterfall.*

Since rushing water can be quite soothing, reduce the stress that's tying your body in knots by standing under a natural waterfall. Let the cool water cascade over your back and shoulders, and feel the anxiety rush away.

FUN FACT

Cascading a remarkable 3,212 feet, Angel Falls in Venezuela is the tallest waterfall in the world. But don't stand under this waterfall!

❏ *192. Tour Hoover Dam.*

Hoover Dam is one of America's great engineering marvels. When it was completed in 1936, it was known as Boulder Dam and was both the world's largest electric-power generating station and the world's largest concrete structure.

(There are now many dams that are larger.) It is located in the Black Canyon of the Colorado River on the border between Arizona and Nevada.

❑ 193. Go on a swamp walk in the Everglades.

Many people think of a swamp as something to avoid. Swamps, however, are amazing ecosystems, and the Everglades in Florida is one of the most spectacular. The next time you're in the Everglades, consider taking a "swamp walk" with an experienced guide. A swamp walk is a great way to see the Everglades' stunning flora and fauna up close, including many plants and animals found nowhere else.

You're going to get dirty, so make certain to bring a change of clothes for the ride home. And bring plenty of mosquito repellent.

❑ 194. Visit all 50 states.

"Fifty nifty United States . . ." was the grade-school song many kids learned back in the 1970s. They're nifty all right, from Seward's Icebox to the tropical paradise of the Aloha State, from Hollywood to New York City, from the Mojave Desert to the Rocky Mountains. What vastness, variety, richness, and beauty are within reach! No language barriers, no border checks (with the exception of crossing Canada to reach Alaska), and a great interstate highway system make this feat a realistic one. (With Hawaii being across the ocean, of course, you may wish to save this state as a grand finale.)

As you travel, consider collecting a souvenir from each state. Some people like to collect souvenir spoons, shot glasses, iron-on patches, pens, key chains, or some other kind of memento. Others may skip the souvenirs and work on completing a map of the United States made from stickers of the various states they visit. Another way to document your travels is to get a picture of yourself at each state's border sign as you enter. (These snapshots also help as you try to remember later in which state you took what pictures.) Each year, plan your vacation around a new group of states until you've seen them all.

❑ 195. Meditate in a Sedona vortex.

Sedona, Arizona, has a long history as a spiritual center. Among its most popular attractions are its vortexes, where people often go to meditate. If this sounds intriguing, consider a trip to Sedona for your next vacation.

❑ 196. Visit the White House.

The White House is much more than just the President's home. It's a signature symbol of America and a must-see destination for all American citizens.

Located at 1600 Pennsylvania Avenue, the White House received its first residents, President John Adams and his wife, Abigail, in 1800. Thomas Jefferson was the first president to open the White House to public tours, and it has stayed open, except during wartime, ever since. On some occasions, however, the crowds have gotten out of control. In 1829, for example, 20,000 Inaugural callers forced President Andrew Jackson to flee the White House while his aides lured the drunken revelers out onto the lawn with tubs of orange juice and whiskey.

Today, public tours of the White House are available for groups of ten or more people. If you'd like to go, a request must be submitted through one of your members of Congress. The requests are accepted up to six months in advance. These self-guided tours are available from 7:30 A.M. to 11 A.M. Tuesday through Thursday, 7:30 A.M. to 12 P.M. on Friday, and 7:30 A.M. to 1 P.M. on Saturday, excluding federal holidays. For current tour information, call 202–456–7041.

❑ 197. Visit the Lincoln Memorial.

"Four score and seven years ago our fathers brought forth on this continent, a new nation, conceived in Liberty, and dedicated to the proposition that all men are created equal." Eloquence was a hallmark of our 16th president. Carved inscriptions of his Second Inaugural Address and his Gettysburg Address grace the north and south chambers of the monument erected in his memory, which stands at the west end of the National Mall in Washington, D.C. The huge statue (19 feet 6 inches) of a seated Lincoln speaks of the greatness of the man himself who helped preserve the Union and put an end to slavery.

■ ■ ■ ■

"In this temple, as in the hearts of the people for whom he saved the Union, the memory of Abraham Lincoln is enshrined forever."

—Lincoln Memorial dedication inscription

■ ■ ■ ■

❑ 198. Climb the stairs to the top of the Washington Monument.

Anyone can ride the elevator to the top of the Washington Monument, but it takes courage (and strong legs) to climb the 555-foot obelisk's 897 steps. Our advice: Hit the gym first.

FUN FACT

The monument commemorates George Washington, the first U.S. president, and it is made of marble, granite, and sandstone. It is the world's tallest stone obelisk and was constructed from 1848 to 1884.

❑ 199. Visit every museum in the Smithsonian Institution.

One of America's greatest treasures is the Smithsonian Institution in Washington, D.C. On your next trip to our nation's capital, make it your goal to visit every museum and gallery—or at least as many as time permits. Among the Smithsonian's most popular attractions are the Smithsonian Institution Building (also known as The Castle), National Museum of American History, National Museum of the American Indian, Freer Gallery of Art, Hirshhorn Museum and Sculpture Garden, National Museum of African Art, National Museum of Natural History, National Portrait Gallery, National Postal Museum, National Air and Space Museum, National Zoological Park, and much, much more. Admission to all Smithsonian museums and the zoo is free.

Seeing all that the Smithsonian has to offer will keep you quite busy. The total number of objects, works of art, and specimens at the Smithsonian is estimated at nearly 137 million, including more than 126 million specimens and artifacts at the National Museum of Natural History.

❏ *200. Visit the Capitol Building and watch Congress in session.*

Since the events of September 11, 2001, you can't just waltz into our nation's Capitol Building and see which senator or congressperson might be roaming the hallways. But you can contact your senator or congressperson, and request a pass to see these elected folks debate the issues on the House or Senate floor. Even if you dislike all politicians on principle, you might be surprised and moved by watching them in action. Whatever they're talking about is likely to affect the folks from Pensacola to Penobscot Bay. Floor debates are a fascinating, protocol-laden process that results in the laws we all live with everyday. Keep in mind that the "real" work of drafting new laws takes place long before the Senate or House floor debate, in committee meetings that have gone on for weeks, months, and, in some cases, years. To watch floor debates: The House and Senate Galleries (the viewing areas) are open to visitors whenever the body is in session, plus the House is open when not in session, as long as it's Monday through Friday, 9:00 A.M. to 4:30 P.M. Passes from your senator or representative are required. Tours of the Capitol are also available, free of charge. You can visit www.visitthecapitol.gov to book a tour, or your congressional representative can arrange one for you.

■ ■ ■ ■

> "Congress is so strange. A man gets up to speak and says nothing. Nobody listens— and then everybody disagrees."
>
> —Boris Marshalov

■ ■ ■ ■

❏ 201. Visit Lexington and Concord in Massachusetts.

See the famous landmarks in Lexington and Concord, where the first battles of the Revolutionary War occurred. Be sure to include in your trip Minute Man National Historical Park and Bunker Hill. And while you're at it, you may want to take a tour of Walden Pond, where Henry David Thoreau wrote his great classic.

❏ 202. Visit the Liberty Bell.

One of the most iconic symbols of American freedom is the Liberty Bell, located in Philadelphia. Every schoolchild has read about it, but like all great symbols, it's best viewed in person.

In 1751, the Pennsylvania Assembly ordered the bell to commemorate the 50th anniversary of William Penn's 1701 Charter of Privileges, Pennsylvania's original constitution. Upon arrival, the bell cracked when it was being tested, and it had to be recast. Officials were dissatisfied with the peal of the second bell and had it recast again. The third bell was hung in the steeple of the State House, and over the years it was rung during historically significant occasions.

The Bell's Current Residence

The Liberty Bell is housed in the Liberty Bell Center, which opened in October 2003. In addition to the bell, visitors can see historic documents and unique images that examine the facts and the myths surrounding the nation's most famous chime.

The Liberty Bell is famous for the large crack that rendered it unringable. Historians believe small cracks had appeared in the bell for years, and that the final expansion that made the bell useless occurred on George Washington's birthday in 1846.

❏ 203. Visit George Washington's Mount Vernon.

FUN FACT

The graves of both George and Martha Washington are located on the grounds of the estate.

Although Washington is the only president not to have lived in the White House, he does have a famous home that countless Americans have toured. Be one of them, and become more familiar with our first president and his wife, Martha.

The Washington family built their home in about 1735. Mount Vernon sits high above the Potomac River in Virginia and is 16 miles south of Washington, D.C. It is open 365 days a year.

❏ 204. Visit Thomas Jefferson's Monticello.

Located near Charlottesville, Virginia, Monticello was the home of Thomas Jefferson, our nation's third president and the primary author of the Declaration of Independence.

A man of many talents, Jefferson designed Monticello, which in Italian means "little mountain." The building was constructed over a period of years, beginning in 1768 and concluding in 1809. It was declared a UNESCO World Heritage Site in 1987.

■ ■ ■ ■

"All tyranny needs to gain a foothold is for people of good conscience to remain silent."

—Thomas Jefferson

■ ■ ■ ■

❑ 205. Visit a U.S. presidential library.

It's become a tradition for U.S. presidents to establish a library to house historic papers and other archives of their years in office. Thirteen presidents currently have libraries across the United States.

Current presidential libraries include:

- ■Herbert Hoover, West Branch, Iowa

- ■Franklin Roosevelt, Hyde Park, New York

- ■Harry Truman, Independence, Missouri

- ■Dwight Eisenhower, Abilene, Kansas

- ■John F. Kennedy, Boston, Massachusetts

- ■Lyndon Johnson, Austin, Texas

NARA

The Office of Presidential Libraries in the National Archives and Records Administration (NARA) oversees the Presidential Library system. When a president leaves office, NARA establishes a presidential project until a new presidential library is built and transferred to the government.

- Richard Nixon, College Park, Maryland, and Yorba Linda, California
- Gerald Ford, Ann Arbor and Grand Rapids, Michigan
- Jimmy Carter, Atlanta, Georgia
- Ronald Reagan, Simi Valley, California
- George Bush, College Station, Texas
- William Clinton, Little Rock, Arkansas
- George W. Bush, Lewisville, Texas

❑ 206. Visit the Kennedy assassination museum in Dallas.

The assassination of President John F. Kennedy on November 22, 1963, was a tragedy that shook the nation. Honor JFK's legacy by visiting the Sixth Floor Museum at Dealy Plaza in Dallas, Texas.

The museum contains more than 35,000 items related to the Kennedy assassination, including original photographs, film and video footage, and other artifacts. Exhibits include the sniper's perch and the staircase where a rifle and clipboard were found, as well as original cameras used by assassination witnesses and a model of Dealy Plaza created by the FBI and used by the Warren Commission.

❑ 207. Visit Plymouth Rock.

Plymouth Rock is, supposedly, the first place the pilgrims set foot off their ship and onto the New World back in 1620. Unfortunately, there's no firm historical evidence to support this. The actual rock has been moved several times over the years. Souvenir hunters have chipped off pieces from it. But even if the Pilgrims' landing rock is uncertain, Plymouth, Massachusetts, is well worth a visit. Plimoth Plantation includes recreated villages of English settlers and Native Americans. The *Mayflower II,* moored there, is a replica of the ship that carried the Pilgrims across the Atlantic Ocean. The town still has the Pilgrims' original churches and a cemetery, where many of the Pilgrims are buried.

❑ *208. Visit Ellis Island.*

Between 1880 and 1930, more than 20 million immigrants streamed into this country through Ellis Island. Today, Ellis Island is an inspirational landmark that has been restored to reflect the immigrant experience, including medical inspection stations, dormitories, and actual items immigrants brought to America.

❑ *209. Attend the Cherokee performance of Trail of Tears.*

A sad and shameful chapter in American history occurred when the United States government removed the Cherokee, Creek, Chickasaw, Seminole, and Choctaw tribes from their native lands and relocated them to a new territory in Oklahoma. The Indian Removal Act was put in place in 1830 and was the legislation used to essentially steal fruitful land from the native tribes and hand it over to settlers. The devastation and hardship the native people endured during their relocation—including cholera and pneumonia—are why they came to refer to the journey as the Trail of Tears. Between 1838 and 1839, as the peaceful Cherokee people were marched 1,000 miles through harsh winters and chilling rain, more than 4,000 died.

In Cherokee, North Carolina, from mid-June to late August, a powerful outdoor drama, *Unto These Hills,* brings to life the tragic history of the Cherokee people on the Trail of Tears. With a cast of 130, the story begins in 1540 and moves through history to the stirring climax of the devastating cross-country march that killed so many along the way. The Great Smoky Mountains provide the backdrop for this 2,800-seat outdoor theater.

❑ 210. Visit the Alamo.

Located in San Antonio, Texas, the Alamo looks smaller in person than it did in the movies. Nevertheless, it's still an inspiring monument to bravery. Meanwhile, San Antonio, an artsy city with a gorgeous downtown river walk, is well worth visiting in its own right.

An Original Survivor

Popular myth says no defender in the Alamo survived the battle, but, in fact, nearly 20 women and children survived. The most famous of these was 22-year-old Susanna Dickinson, who was released by the Mexican general Santa Anna, carrying a warning to Sam Houston to surrender.

❑ 211. Visit the adobe homes in Taos Pueblo, New Mexico.

Taos is a Native American village that has preserved the original residences of people descended from the Anasazi nation. The adobe homes are a fascinating look at what life was like for these proud people. For a better understanding of America's past, Taos Pueblo is a must-see.

❏ 212. Visit Gettysburg National Military Park.

The Civil War was a dark period in American history, and the Battle of Gettysburg was a defining moment in that conflict. Gettysburg National Military Park honors those involved and should be a required visit for every American.

Fought over three days in July 1863, the Battle of Gettysburg

Lincoln's Gettysburg Address

Contrary to popular belief, Abraham Lincoln did not hurriedly write the Gettysburg Address on the back of an envelope. In truth, it was a speech to which he devoted quite a bit of time, even though it lasted just a couple of minutes.

was an important turning point in the Civil War in that it halted Confederate General Robert E. Lee's invasion of the North and forced his army to retreat back into Virginia—a loss the South was never able to overcome. But the consequences of the battle were horrific: There were 51,000 combined casualties, and most of those who died were buried on farmland throughout the tiny Virginia crossroads town.

Gettysburg National Military Park offers a variety of sights and activities, including guided tours, battlefield walks, and evening campfire programs during the summer. Also of interest is the Gettysburg National Military Park Museum and Visitor Center, and the David Wills House, where Lincoln stayed prior to giving his famous speech.

❏ 213. Visit the Birmingham Civil Rights Institute.

If you want to catch a memorable glimpse of the civil rights struggle of African Americans, go to Birmingham, Alabama, and tour the museum and performance center of the Birmingham Civil Rights Institute.

FUN FACT

The 16th Street Baptist Church was the first black church to be organized in Birmingham. The Birmingham Civil Rights Institute displays an exhibition of this historic church.

Birmingham had a vital role in the civil rights movement, and many of the stories are recorded in words and photos at the Institute. You will gain significant insights into American history.

❏ 214. Visit Ground Zero in New York.

There are only a few places on Earth that have become sacred ground for Americans because of what happened there: Normandy Beach, the Gettysburg battlefield, and now Ground Zero, the site of the 2001 terrorist attack on the World Trade Center (WTC) in New York City. To see the site in person is to be struck by the enormity of what happened there.

Begin your pilgrimage with a walk around the 16-acre site on the fenced walkway that surrounds it, from which you can watch the ongoing construction of the 1,776-foot One World Trade Center at the heart of the new World Trade Center Complex. Then visit the Tribute World Trade Center visitor's center, where five galleries depict the WTC as it once was, the events that unfolded on 9/11, the rescue and recovery operations, the lives of those who were lost, and the stories of those who have turned their grief into action through volunteer activities around the world. With changing exhibits, audio narratives, and artifacts recovered from the site, the center is a monument to the heroism and the tragedy of that day.

■ ■ ■ ■

"Courage is the first of human qualities because it is the quality which guarantees the others."

—Winston Churchill

■ ■ ■ ■

❑ 215. Ring in the New Year in Times Square.

FUN FACT

The Times Square New Year's Eve Ball is a 12-foot geodesic globe covered with 2,668 Waterford Crystals. It weighs 11,875 pounds.

Every year, hundreds of thousands of people ring in the New Year in New York's Times Square. At least once, you should be part of the crowd.

The ball first fell in Times Square in 1904. Since then, the event has become an annual tradition. Superstar musical acts provide entertainment, and more than a ton of confetti rains down at the stroke of midnight.

If you go, arrive early and dress warmly. The temperatures can get frigid.

❑ 216. Enjoy a hot dog at Nathan's in New York.

Hot dog joints are everywhere in New York City, but there's only one Nathan's. The next time you're in the Big Apple, grab a dog at the original Nathan's on Coney Island.

FUN FACT

Nathan's has been holding its hot dog-eating contest since 1916. Competitors come from around the world. In 2009, Joey Chestnut of San Jose, California, barely defeated Takeru Kobayashi of Japan by consuming 68 hot dogs in ten minutes to walk away with his third Mustard Yellow Belt. The diminutive Kobayashi had won the contest a record six times before Chestnut began his reign.

❑ 217. Go ice skating at Rockefeller Center.

The next time you're in New York City during the winter, go ice skating at the world-famous Rockefeller Plaza. You'll feel like a kid again, if only for a few minutes.

218. Visit the Metropolitan Museum of Art in New York City.

New York City rivals Washington, D.C., when it comes to amazing museums. One of the Big Apple's most famous and influential is the Metropolitan Museum of Art, whose collections include more than two million works spanning 5,000 years.

You'll find all the great masters there, from Degas to Vermeer, in addition to exquisite works from prehistory through the modern age. So large is the museum's permanent collection that it loans more than 5,000 works to other museums and cultural institutions each year.

The Metropolitan Museum of Art is a feast for the eyes and the soul. The next time you're in town, check it out.

■ ■ ■ ■

"Every great work of art has two faces, one toward its own time and one toward the future, toward eternity."

—Daniel Barenboim

■ ■ ■ ■

219. Visit the American Museum of Natural History.

From massive dinosaurs to tiny hummingbirds, you'll find it all—and more—at the American Museum of Natural

History in New York City. For first-time visitors, education has never been more fun!

Perhaps not surprisingly, the museum's most popular exhibits are its Fossil Halls, two of which are devoted to dinosaurs. Other permanent exhibits include:

- Culture Halls
- Mammal Halls
- The Hall of Biodiversity
- The Hall of Gems
- Bird Halls
- Dioramas

After you've seen those exhibits, make sure you check out the Lefrak IMAX Theater and the famous Hayden Planetarium. For information on all that the museum has to offer, visit www.amnh.org.

❑ 220. Visit the Statue of Liberty.

The Statue of Liberty was a gift from the people of France and stands as a sentinel on Liberty Island at the mouth of the Hudson River in New York Harbor. She defines America's founding principle of freedom for all. Every American should visit her at least once.

FUN FACT

The Statue of Liberty was dedicated on October 28, 1886, commemorating the centennial of the signing of the United States Declaration of Independence.

Frédéric Auguste Bartholdi sculpted the statue, which is 151 feet tall, but with the pedestal and foundation, the sculpture is 305 feet tall.

221. Ride the Staten Island Ferry.

FUN FACT

Each year, 20 million people ride the ferry.

One of the best ways to view the majesty of New York City is to ride the Staten Island Ferry from Staten Island to Manhattan. This remarkable view of the Big Apple is priceless.

222. Enjoy the view from the observation deck on the Empire State Building.

Going up? Yup—102 stories up! This Art Deco skyscraper is a New York City hallmark and a must-do attraction for visitors. After the collapse of the World Trade Center (WTC) towers in 2001, the Empire State Building once again stands as New York's tallest building. It had held the distinction of being the world's tallest building for more than 40 years from its completion in 1931, until WTC's North Tower was completed in 1972. Today, the only taller skyscraper in the United States is Chicago's Willis Tower (formerly the Sears Tower).

Since its opening, more than 110 million people have visited the observation decks of the Empire State

FUN FACT

In 1964, floodlights were added to illuminate the top of the building at night. Colors are selected to correspond with seasons, holidays, and events.

Building. On the 86th floor, people can enjoy impressive 360-degree views of the city. A second observation deck is on the top floor and is open again to the public after a closure between 1999 and 2005. Today, it is completely enclosed and much smaller than the original observation area. There is a fee for visiting the 86th floor, and an additional fee for going up to the 102nd. And though the lines are long, for an extra fee, tourists can advance to the front of the line.

☐ 223. Enjoy the view from the Willis Tower in Chicago.

The United States offers numerous opportunities to enjoy the view from very high places. One of the most striking is the observation deck of the Willis Tower (formerly known as the Sears Tower) in Chicago. If you've never been there, make it a must-see part of your next vacation.

> **FUN FACT**
>
> The Willis Tower was the tallest building in the world for 25 years, until the construction of the Petronas Towers in Kuala Lampur, Malaysia, in 1998.

At 110 stories, the Willis Tower, located on Wacker Drive in the middle of the West Loop, is the tallest building in North America. It rises 1,450 feet above the Chicago skyline, and contains 3.8 million rentable square feet of space. The Willis Tower Skydeck is a very popular tourist attraction, along with its awesome new ledge. On a clear day, you can see 40 to 50 miles—all the way to nearby states. For a sight you'll never forget, arrive at the Skydeck about 45 minutes before dusk and watch the sun set on the horizon.

224. Visit the Illinois Holocaust Museum and Education Center near Chicago.

Who can forget the movie *Schindler's List,* which brought to life, for the first time to some of us, the powerful and heartbreaking realities of the Holocaust? In Skokie, Illinois, just north of Chicago, such recollections are built into its world-class Holocaust Museum and Education Center. The museum's mission is dedication "to preserving the memories of those lost in the Holocaust and teaching current generations about the need to fight hatred, indifference and genocide in today's world."

The Zev and Shifra Karkomi Permanent Exhibit in the museum is for visitors 12 years of age and older. More than 500 artifacts, documents, and photos accompany the historical timeline from prewar German life, to ghetto life and concentration camps, and finally to liberation and resettlement. The site also hosts a railway car like those into which Jews were crammed and transported to Nazi deportation programs.

225. Enjoy the view from atop the St. Louis Arch.

St. Louis, Missouri, is known for a lot of things, but it's perhaps best known as the home of the Gateway Arch. When traveling through the Show Me State, take an hour to enjoy the view from the monument's observation deck. Enclosed trams take visitors to the top of the Arch every ten minutes, traveling at a breakneck four miles per hour. Along the way, you'll be treated to a narration of the Arch's history. Afterward, visit the exhibits in each leg of the Arch.

The Gateway Arch is a popular attraction. To avoid the crowds, go before 10 A.M.

A Sturdy Edifice

At 630 feet, the Gateway Arch is the tallest monument in the United States. Because of its unique design, it can safely sway a maximum of 18 inches in a 150-mile-per-hour wind. During periods of relative calm, its usual sway is just half an inch.

❑ 226. Visit the Frank Lloyd Wright Home and Studio.

Frank Lloyd Wright was not only a great architect but also a fascinating person. You can discover both the architect and the person when you tour his home and studio in Oak Park, Illinois. As a bonus, you can see several homes Wright built in his neighborhood; they are indicated in a brochure at the bookstore that adjoins his house.

FUN FACT

In 1991, the American Institute of Architects recognized Frank Lloyd Wright as "the greatest American architect of all time."

❑ 227. Walk or bike across the Golden Gate Bridge.

People photograph the Golden Gate from every angle imaginable, but the best angle is from the bridge itself while walking or biking across. The bridge is 1.7 miles long, and it's easy to take a picture while traveling in either direction. Bike rental companies are located nearby; walking and biking are restricted, however, during certain hours of the day.

❑ 228. *Take a cable-car ride in San Francisco.*

San Francisco's famed cable cars are a great way to see the city, from Fisherman's Wharf to Nob Hill and Ghirardelli Square, and from the financial district to Chinatown.

A young Englishman proposed cable cars as a way to avoid more tragedies on those steep slopes, such as horses being dragged to their deaths when they couldn't navigate the slippery cobblestones. In 1873, cable cars were first tested in San

FUN FACT

In 1998, Fannie Mae Barnes became the first woman to operate a cable car, having developed the upper body strength it takes to operate the cable grip. She was 52 at the time.

Francisco. Although the cable cars fell out of favor in the 1950s, full service was restored in the 1980s. Today, there are three cable car routes in operation, including one that runs over Nob Hill, where the very first cable car system was tested.

❑ 229. *Tour Alcatraz Island.*

If you ever visit San Francisco, it may not occur to you—with all there is to do in that fascinating city—to check out Alcatraz. This former prison was built on a gigantic rock—a tiny island in the San Francisco Bay with its churning waters whose temperature averages 50–55 degrees F. Alcatraz, which means "sea birds," was originally used as a military fortress during the Civil War, with troops permanently assigned to it in 1859. But

from 1934 to 1963, it served as a federal penitentiary. Its more famous residents included Al "Scarface" Capone and the "Birdman" Robert Stroud, both made famous by films about the prison.

❑ 230. Visit the Hearst Castle.

William Randolph Hearst was a man whose dreams were as vast as his fortune. Eager to live in a palace as grand as those he saw in Europe as a child, he built the Hearst Castle in San Simeon, California. It's a tribute to opulence like no other, and something that must be seen to be believed.

Designed by architect Julia Morgan, the Hearst Castle was built over a period of 28 years and contains approximately 160 rooms and

FUN FACT

The film *Citizen Kane*, written by and starring Orson Welles, was based in large part on William Randolph Hearst.

127 acres of gardens, terraces, pools, and walkways. It also houses a good portion of Hearst's museum-quality art collection.

❑ 231. *Take a stroll down Rodeo Drive in Beverly Hills.*

Care to see how the other half lives? Take a stroll down posh Rodeo Drive, where the rich and famous shop. The renowned stretch of stores and boutiques is just three blocks long, but it contains some of the most famous names in luxury and opulence, including Cartier, Tiffany, Neiman Marcus, Christian Dior, Gucci, and Saks Fifth Avenue, just to name a few. The district begins at Wilshire Boulevard in the south and runs north to Santa Monica Boulevard, where it turns into an affluent residential neighborhood.

When you visit, just remember: If you have to ask the price, you probably can't afford it.

❑ 232. *Visit the Biltmore.*

If the Hearst Castle in California epitomizes opulence, the Biltmore estate in Asheville, North Carolina, is its East Coast equivalent. And like the Hearst Castle, it's a marvel to behold. Built between 1888 and 1895 as a country retreat for George and Edith Vanderbilt, the Biltmore is now both a hotel and a popular tourist destination. Sitting on 8,000 acres in western North Carolina, the French Renaissance château—and America's largest privately-owned home—exudes luxury and is almost as much a museum as it is a place of residence. Among its treasures are original art from greats such as Renoir, 16th-century tapestries,

Napoleon's chess set, and a library containing more than 10,000 volumes.

The Biltmore also features a stunning banquet hall with a 70-foot ceiling, 65 fireplaces, an indoor pool, a bowling alley, numerous antiques, and acres of gardens that are beyond compare. Designed by renowned landscape architect Frederick Law Olmsted, the rose garden contains more than 250 different varieties.

❑ 233. Take a photo on the Walk of Fame in Hollywood.

There's a place in California where you can reach for the stars by touching the sidewalk. You'll find it along Hollywood Boulevard from Gower Street to La Brea Avenue and on Vine Street from Yucca Street to Sunset Boulevard. An online search easily turns up specific locations on the sidewalks of the names of your favorite film stars.

❑ 234. Attend the Rose Parade.

Every New Year's Day, an estimated one million people attend the Rose Parade in Pasadena, California. Next year, make it one million and one!

The Rose Parade is one of the most-watched events of its kind in the world, attracting a television audience of nearly 40 million Americans. It follows a 5.5-mile winding route and is famous for its flower-festooned floats. You don't need tickets to attend the Rose Parade unless you prefer a grandstand seat. It's suggested, however, that you arrive early because people begin camping out along the route at noon the day before.

The First Rose Parade

The Rose Parade began in 1890 as a celebration of California's mild winter climate. It was patterned after the "Battle of the Flowers" in Nice, France. The first parade was a modest procession of flower-covered carriages, followed by an afternoon of games, including tug-of-war and sack races.

❑ 235. Attend the Macy's Thanksgiving Day Parade.

FUN FACT

The floats and balloons in the Macy's Thanksgiving Day Parade are in the daily parades at the Universal Studios theme park in Orlando.

Every Thanksgiving, Macy's department store sponsors a parade that has become a favorite of the citizens of New York City. Once you attend this parade, it will probably become your best-loved as well. The parade begins at 9 A.M. and lasts for three hours.

❑ 236. Renew your wedding vows in Las Vegas.

Marriage isn't always a sure bet. In fact, sometimes it's a real gamble. But if your spouse is a winner, why not renew your vows in Las Vegas?

There are a lot of funky little wedding chapels in Vegas, where getting remarried can be more of a show than a ceremony. For example, how would you like an Elvis impersonator to officiate

over your vows? Las Vegas is probably the only city in the country where something like that is not only tolerated but encouraged.

❏ 237. *Drive through Palm Beach in a convertible.*

You don't have to be rich to feel rich. The next time you're in South Florida, rent a convertible and drive through ritzy Palm Beach. To really look like you live there, wear sunglasses and an ascot. Wave to strangers as if you know them.

■ ■ ■ ■

"Being rich is having money; being wealthy is having time."

—Margaret Bonnano

■ ■ ■ ■

❏ 238. *Visit Disneyland with kids.*

In July 1955, Walt Disney wisely decided to cast his magic in Southern California by putting Disneyland in Anaheim. The first Disney theme park contained four major areas that included Tomorrowland, Frontierland, Adventureland, and Main Street, USA, with their own unique attractions.

Disneyland was built for kids and kids at heart, so for more fun, be sure to take children with you. At Disneyland,

you will see your favorite Disney characters, with dining opportunities that range from fast food to gourmet restaurants. Make sure you bring your camera—these are memories you'll want to keep forever.

❑ 239. Go to Disney World without children.

If you think Disney World is just for kids, you haven't been there lately. These days, the Magic Kingdom is just one small part of this sprawling vacation destination. You could take two different approaches to going there without children. You could try catering to your inner child and head to the Magic Kingdom and do all the things you're supposed to be too old to do—careen down Splash Mountain, sail with the Pirates of the Caribbean, and have your picture taken with Mickey.

Or for another approach, you could just focus on the more adult entertainment options: the Boardwalk, a recreation of 1930s Atlantic City; Downtown Disney, a shopping and entertainment Mecca; resort hotels—more than 20 of them—with themes ranging from Disney's All-Star Music Resort to Disney's Yacht Club Resort; and several locations for golf and tennis. Of course, there are also

Disney's other theme parks—Epcot, Disney's Hollywood Studios, the Animal Kingdom Park, and the Wide World of Sports Complex—all of which are just as much fun for adults as for kids. There are also special events for adults throughout the year, such as the International Food & Wine Festival and International Flower & Garden Festival (both held at Epcot) and "ESPN The Weekend" at Disney's Hollywood Studios Theme Park.

❏ *240. Witness a rocket launch at Cape Canaveral.*

For a truly awesome, once-in-a-lifetime experience, be on hand to watch a rocket lift off from the Kennedy Space Center at Cape Canaveral, Florida. Though the viewing area is miles away from the launch pad, the tremendous power of these enormous space-faring beasts will literally make your sternum vibrate.

> ### Launch Sites
> All space shuttles launch from the Kennedy Space Center, but that isn't NASA's only launch site; rockets also take off from Vandenberg Air Force Base in California. In addition, NASA has secondary launch sites at Kodiak Island, Alaska, and the Kwajalein Atoll in the Republic of the Marshall Islands.

If your dream is to watch a space shuttle launch, you'd better hurry; NASA plans to mothball the decades-old shuttle fleet in 2010, and its replacement likely won't be ready before 2015. Plenty of other rockets, however, most of them carrying satellites and other important scientific equipment, lift off from Cape Canaveral on a regular basis.

(Visit www.nasa.gov/missions for the latest schedule.) While you're there, make sure you take a tour of the Space Center and visit the Rocket Garden and other attractions. On most days you can also attend a public lecture by a veteran astronaut, so bring your questions—and your camera!

❑ 241. Visit the Munster Mansion.

If you're a fan of *The Munsters*, that zany '60s sitcom featuring Herman and Lily Munster, make plans to visit the real-life Munster Mansion in Waxahachie, Texas. The 5,825-square-foot replica of the Munsters' television home is the private residence of Sandra and Charles McKee. They studied all 70 episodes of the classic comedy to get the layout just right.

The McKees open up their home to tours only in October, when they host an annual Halloween Charity Event that often brings in *Munsters* cast members such as Pat Priest and Butch Patrick. It's okay, however, to take photos of the house anytime from outside the gate.

For further information about the Munster Mansion, visit www.munstermansion.com.

❑ 242. Visit Metropolis, Illinois—Superman's hometown.

The mythical city of Metropolis is where Superman plied his superhero trade, and the real town of Metropolis, Illinois, has taken full advantage of his fame. The main attraction is the Superman Museum, featuring memorabilia from the many versions of the Man of Steel, including the original costumes from the 1950s television series and the device used to make George Reeves "fly."

❏ 243. Attend San Diego's Comic-Con.

You don't have to be a pop culture geek to enjoy Comic-Con International, but it doesn't hurt. Held annually at the San Diego Convention Center, Comic-Con is the largest comic book/movie convention in the world, drawing more than 125,000 devoted fans. As a result, it has become THE event for movie studios to promote their upcoming big-budget films; positive word-of-mouth at a sneak-peek can translate into big bucks at the box office. There's also a vendors' room and costume contest.

Think of Comic-Con as the geek equivalent of Mecca: Every fan should make a pilgrimage there at least once in his or her life.

❏ 244. Look for aliens in Roswell, New Mexico.

Flying saucers have been reported throughout the United States for decades, but no town has capitalized on the phenomenon like Roswell, New Mexico. On your next vacation, visit Roswell for your own close encounter of the third kind. (Alien contact not guaranteed.)

Roswell has been ground zero for UFO investigators since July 7, 1947, when it was reported that a UFO had crashed there and that both debris and alien bodies had been recovered. Military officials claim that the crashed object was really a classified high-altitude surveillance balloon, but UFO conspiracy theorists maintain that this explanation is merely a cover-up.

❏ 245. Go up the Space Needle in Seattle.

With its 360-degree view and an observation deck 520 feet off the ground, the Space Needle provides plenty of elevation to give you a view you'll not soon forget (on a clear day, of course). To the west lie the Olympic Mountains and Puget Sound, while to the east the Cascade Range (including Mount Rainier) is visible.

Needle Nuts and Bolts

- The Space Needle was built for the 1962 World's Fair.
- At its highest point, it's 605 feet tall; at its widest it's 138 feet across; it weighs 9,550 tons.
- It is built to withstand winds of up to 200 mph (320 km/h) and earthquakes up to a magnitude of 9.5.
- There are 25 lightning rods on its roof to prevent lightning damage.
- The topmost of the tower's two restaurants—SkyCity—slowly rotates for a full view of the city as you dine.

❑ 246. Take the Seattle Underground Tour.

Did you know that the city of Seattle is actually built on top of old Seattle? On your next trip to Seattle, be sure to take a tour that will tell the city's history and show some of the old shops and streets that were at ground level prior to the 1889 fire that destroyed 33 city blocks.

FUN FACT

Two years after the city condemned the underground structures, which had been buried by mudslides, the 1909 World's Fair took place in Seattle.

❑ 247. Visit the original Boys Town in Omaha.

The first Boys Town, located near Omaha, Nebraska, provides a caring environment for troubled or abandoned youngsters. Its success is a tribute to one man's dream, and the original Boys Town Village is well worth a visit when you're in the area.

In 1917, Father Edward Flanagan founded Boys Town, which originally was a small home for homeless boys. It has grown into a nationwide organization with sites in a dozen states and the District of Columbia, and it is now home to both boys and girls. Its national youth care and health programs aid an estimated 51,000 children each year.

FUN FACT

Spencer Tracy won an Academy Award for his portrayal of Edward Flanagan in the film *Boys Town* (1938).

❑ 248. Visit the United States Space Camp in Huntsville, Alabama.

The U.S. Space & Rocket Center offers a wonderful live-in experience at its Space Camp in Huntsville. Both

FUN FACT

Chelsea Clinton attended U.S. Space Camp during Bill Clinton's first term.

adults and youths can reside at this camp and expand their knowledge of science, engineering, aviation, and exploration. There are a variety of programs designed for various age groups.

❑ 249. Participate in an authentic Hawaiian luau.

Grass skirts, roasted pig, and tiki torches—what else comes to mind as you think of a luau? What you may not know about this traditional Hawaiian celebration is that it wasn't always called a luau, but rather *'aha 'aina*. These ancient celebrations marked significant events, such as warriors returning from battle, homecomings from long journeys, a child's coming of age, and so on. The term *luau* didn't come into use until 1819 when King Kamehameha II abolished traditional religious practices that forbade women from eating with men at the feasts. The king boldly broke these long-standing taboos by inviting the women to join him at a special feast. A main chicken dish called "Luau" was served, and the name became synonymous with the new tradition.

Hawaii offers numerous commercial luau productions. These generally include dinner with many traditional foods and Hawaiian or Polynesian dance performances. Some hotels host luaus, and, as weather permits, these outdoor events have a view of the setting sun over the water. Some luaus, however, are held at private locations. To find the luau you're looking for, ask at your hotel and check with the locals. After you make your reservations, get ready to eat with abandon, and watch the dancers perform some amazing hula moves.

❏ 250. *Visit Father Damien's memorial on Molokai.*

In 1865, white settlers persuaded King Kamehameha V to remove native Hawaiians who were suffering from Hansen's disease, commonly known as leprosy, to a settlement on the island of Molokai. They were isolated from all contact with the rest of society and treated inhumanely. Religious leaders argued that their disease was evidence of moral impurity, and thus they deserved to be banished, though many of them were only babies.

Father Damien, on the other hand, felt that they deserved God's mercy, and so he went there to minister to their needs. His remarkable ministry did much to help these people. Today, the Kalaupapa settlement is a United States National Historical Park and can be visited by riding mules down a steep mountain.

FUN FACT

In October 2009, the Roman Catholic Church held a lavish ceremony honoring Father Damien, a priest from Belgium, as a saint.

251. Take a helicopter ride over one of the Hawaiian islands.

With its lush forests, sunny beaches, and inspiring waterfalls, Hawaii is every tourist's dream. But why look at it from the ground when you can revel in its majestic beauty from a helicopter? It's a dream that's easy to realize. No matter where you stay in Hawaii, you're almost certain to find companies that offer helicopter tours of the region's most dazzling sights. Of course, a helicopter ride isn't cheap, but once you're in the air, you'll find it's worth every penny.

252. Attend the Albuquerque International Balloon Fiesta.

Every October, the skies over Albuquerque, New Mexico, come alive with colorful hot-air balloons. It's all part of the Albuquerque International Balloon Fiesta, an annual event that draws crowds from around the world.

The Fiesta started in 1972 with just 19 hot-air balloons. Today, an estimated 700 take flight over 365-acre Balloon Fiesta Park. In addition to balloons, the event features food and a variety of fun activities. For information on the next International Balloon Fiesta, visit www.balloonfiesta.com.

❑ 253. Visit the Guggenheim Museum in New York.

Housed in a building designed by esteemed architect Frank Lloyd Wright, the Solomon R. Guggenheim Museum in Manhattan's Upper East Side is one of the most important museums of modern art in the world—and a dream destination for every art lover.

The works found within the Guggenheim cover a broad array of styles and include some of the world's finest examples of abstract and Surrealist painting and sculpture; Impressionist and Post-Impressionist masterpieces; and European and American Minimalist, Post-Minimalist, Environmental, and Conceptual art.

What the Guggenheim Has to Offer

The Guggenheim is much more than just an art museum. It also offers special exhibitions, lectures by renowned artists and critics, performances and film screenings, as well as classes for teens and adults.

So put aside your preconceived notions of what art is and open your mind to a remarkable new experience by visiting the Guggenheim Museum, which opened its doors on October 21, 1959. You won't be sorry.

❑ 254. Attend the Sundance Film Festival.

The Sundance Film Festival in Utah is one of the most prestigious cinema events in the world, and it attracts some of the biggest names in the industry. But you don't have to be a film star or hotshot director to attend—the festival is open to everyone.

In most cases, attending a screening, panel discussion, or other event is as simple as purchasing a ticket. Of course, some of the more popular movies may sell out, so you should get to the box office early. If you'd like to see several films, the purchase of a multi-ticket package is recommended.

FUN FACT

In 1978, the Sundance Film Festival started in Salt Lake City as the Utah/U.S. Film Festival. One of its key founders is actor Robert Redford.

❑ 255. Over the course of a weekend, watch the ten "best" movies ever made.

In 1997, the American Film Institute announced its list of the 100 best films from the first 100 years of movie making (1896–1996). The top ten are *Citizen Kane, Casablanca, The Godfather, Gone with the Wind, Lawrence of Arabia, The Wizard of Oz, The Graduate, On the Waterfront, Schindler's List,* and *Singin' in the Rain.* If you watched them all from start to finish, it would be a 20-hour marathon. If you added in breaks for eating, sleeping, and visiting the restroom, you could accomplish the task over a weekend and still have time to make the popcorn.

❑ *256. Watch every Academy Award–winning Best Picture from the past ten years.*

Since 1927, one film has annually been honored with an Oscar for the Best Picture of the Year. To watch all of these movies would take a very long time. You can make it your life's goal, or you can just take on the last ten.

❑ *257. Watch a Busby Berkeley musical.*

No one could choreograph a dance sequence like the legendary Busby Berkeley. If you've never watched one of his films, rent *Gold Diggers of 1937*—it's one of his best!

■　■　■　■

"I wanted to make people happy, if only for an hour."

—Busby Berkeley

■　■　■　■

❑ *258. Watch Boris Karloff play the Frankenstein monster.*

In the view of many horror buffs, the best Frankenstein flicks are the three starring Boris Karloff as the creature:

Frankenstein (1931), *Bride of Frankenstein* (1935), and *Son of Frankenstein* (1939). For some great thrills, watch them back to back.

W. H. Pratt

Boris Karloff was born William Henry Pratt in London, England, on November 23, 1887. He later moved to Canada and took Boris Karloff as his professional moniker. Karloff died on February 2, 1969.

❑ 259. Watch every Alfred Hitchcock movie.

Critics call Alfred Hitchcock "the master of suspense," and rightfully so. This year, make a commitment to watch every thriller the British director made—all 66 of them! The list begins with *The Lodger* (1926) and concludes with *Family Plot* (1976).

■ ■ ■ ■

"I am a typed director. If I made Cinderella, the audience would immediately be looking for a body in the coach."

—Alfred Hitchcock

■ ■ ■ ■

❑ 260. Watch every James Bond movie.

The James Bond series is one of the most successful and longest-running movie franchises in history. Schedule a long weekend to watch all 24 Bond movies back to back. Midway through, stop for a vodka martini—shaken, not stirred.

There have been 22 "official" Bond movies and two independent productions to date. The series started in 1962 with *Dr. No*, starring Sean Connery as Ian Flemings's no-nonsense master spy. The most recent entry is 2008's *Quantum of Solace*, starring Daniel Craig. A total of seven actors have portrayed Bond in motion pictures, eight if you count David Niven in the 1967 parody film *Casino Royale*.

> **FUN FACT**
>
> In addition to James Bond, Ian Fleming penned the popular children's book *Chitty Chitty Bang Bang*.

❑ 261. Visit Tinseltown and look for film stars.

Go to Hollywood, the movie capital of the world, take an evening stroll, and see how many film celebrities you can spot. Hint: Screaming paparazzi and flashbulbs are a dead giveaway.

Hollywood is a district in Los Angeles and not far from downtown L.A. In 1910, D. W. Griffith shot the first film in Hollywood. It was *In Old California*.

❑ 262. Visit Grauman's Chinese Theatre.

No trip to Hollywood would be complete without a visit to Grauman's Chinese Theatre on Hollywood Boulevard. For more than 80 years, some of show biz's greatest luminaries have trod its red carpet.

Built in 1927 at a cost of $2 million, Grauman's Chinese Theatre (so named because of the Chinese theme to its decor) opened its doors on May 18, 1927, with the premiere of Cecil B. DeMille's *The King of Kings*. Riots broke out as throngs of people wrangled to see the stars who turned out for the grand opening. Grauman's remains a popular venue for motion picture premieres.

The First Footprints

One of the most popular attractions at Grauman's Chinese Theatre is its collection of celebrity handprints and footprints set in concrete. According to the Theatre's account, Mary Pickford and Douglas Fairbanks were the first to leave their footprints.

❑ 263. Attend a taping of Saturday Night Live.

The hottest ticket in New York City isn't the latest Broadway hit; it's for a taping of *Saturday Night Live* (*SNL*). If you're a fan, there's no greater thrill than sitting in the audience of this groundbreaking comedy show.

There are two ways to get tickets to *SNL*. The first is through an e-mail lottery established by NBC, which is held every August. Your chances, however, of actually being selected are slim. A better alternative is to get in line at 30 Rockefeller Plaza early on the day of the show and hope for a standby ticket for either the 8 P.M. dress rehearsal or the 11:30 live show.

❏ 264. See a Broadway show.

Broadway has been called the longest street in America—if you include all the Broadway productions mounted across the country each year.

> **TKTS**
>
> Pinching pennies? Stop by the TKTS ticket booths in Times Square for same-day discount tickets to Broadway shows, Off-Broadway shows, and other events. You might find them at half-off! The line at the TKTS booth gets long, of course, but it moves quickly. The best deals are for the older shows. You can often score a real bargain as theaters try to fill empty seats toward the end of the day. Go to www.nytix.com for the complete scoop.

Of course, there's nothing like seeing a Broadway show on Broadway, including the opportunity to see some of your favorite performers in person.

❏ 265. Attend a live theater production of a Shakespeare play.

You've heard the famous lines "To be, or not to be" and "To thine own self be true" but have you ever immersed yourself in a live production of *Hamlet?* Perhaps you're a bit put off by the prospect of wading through Shakespeare's "thees," "thous," "canst nots," and other such archaic words and expressions. Lo, fear thee not! It's something that can be surmounted.

Reading the play in advance (with the goal of getting the gist of the story, rather than trying to understand every word or expression) is an advisable first step before attending a Shakespeare play. Another way to prepare for the theater is renting a modern movie production of the play and watching it.

Being able to see actors up close will help you interpret some of what you may not have understood while you were reading the play. (It's during this viewing that you'll likely catch some of Shakespeare's wonderful humor.) With these preparations, you are ready to be carried away in one of the great playwright's histories, comedies, or tragedies that reveal his genius. Summertime often brings some great outdoor Shakespeare productions to town. Check the Arts or Events listings in your local newspaper.

Now, a history, tragedy, or comedy? That is the question.

❑ 266. Participate in a community play.

If you've ever had the urge to release your inner ham, now's the time to do it. These days, there are community theater groups in every big city and in many tiny hamlets in America. Don't think you have the talent? Don't worry about it. Community theater groups need all kinds of help, not just actors; set design, costumes, lighting, and publicity are just a few of the tasks required to put on a show. In fact, many theater groups will require you to pitch in with those tasks whether you have a leading role or are just a walk-on. And that's part of the fun—it's all about community, after all—spending time with new and old friends and creating something together. It may turn out to be a popular hit or a total flop, but it's sure to be a lot of fun along the way. To find a community theater group in your area, go to www.aact.org, the Web site of the American Association of Community Theater—or just ask around.

❏ *267. Join a local book club.*

If you're an avid reader, share your passion by joining a local book club. It's a great way to make new friends and enjoy a common interest with kindred souls.

Book clubs have become increasingly popular in recent years. The premise is simple: Everyone agrees to read the same book, then meet on a designated date to discuss the book and share their observations and insights. Some book clubs meet in book stores or restaurants, while others meet in members' homes. Consult your local library or book store for book clubs in your area. If none exist, consider starting one.

❑ 268. Make a list of all the books you've wanted to read.

Are you just too busy to read a good book? Then you must make the time. Create a list of all of the books you've been dying to read, prioritize them, then devote a block of time each day just for reading. It doesn't have to be a big block of time; 30 minutes to an hour is fine. Use your lunch hour or that quiet time before you go to bed. Be adamant that this is your reading time, and don't let anything interfere. You'll be amazed at how much reading you get done—and how much you enjoy it.

❑ 269. Read all of Edgar Rice Burroughs's Tarzan or Mars novels.

No one could write an adventure story like Edgar Rice Burroughs! Relive your wonder years by reading either all 24 of ERB's Tarzan novels or all 11 volumes of his Mars series.

Tarzan of the Apes debuted in the October 1912 issue of *The All-Story Magazine* and was first published as a novel in 1914. It was a remarkable success, and Tarzan quickly became one of literature's best-known fictional characters, as well as a cinema icon.

Burroughs's Mars, or Barsoom, novels, featuring Virginian adventurer John Carter, are the author's second most popular series. It begins with *A Princess of Mars*

(1917), which was first serialized as *Under the Moons of Mars* in *The All-Story Magazine* in 1912 (prior to the first appearance of Tarzan), and concludes with *John Carter of Mars,* a collection of stories first published in book form in 1964.

❑ *270. Read a classic novel.*

Remember all those books you had to read in 10th grade, such as *Silas Marner, Pride and Prejudice,* and *Oliver Twist?* Many of them are actually great reads, even if they seemed tedious back then. As an adult, you may find classic novels to be surprisingly relevant, moving, and even funny.

■ ■ ■ ■

"Literature adds to reality, it does not simply describe it. It enriches the necessary competencies that daily life requires and provides; and in this respect, it irrigates the deserts that our lives have already become."

—C. S. Lewis

■ ■ ■ ■

❏ 271. Read every Pulitzer Prize– winning novel from the previous ten years.

More than 80 novels have received the Pulitzer Prize for Literature, including such literary classics as *The Grapes of Wrath* (1940), *All the King's Men* (1947), and *To Kill a Mockingbird* (1961), along with more popular fare such as *Gone with the Wind* (1937). Reading the entire list could be a lifetime chore, but you should be able to handle the last ten years. Depending on when you start, that would include: *The Amazing Adventures of Kavalier & Clay* by Michael Chabon, 2001 (based on the early years of the comic book industry); *Empire Falls* by Richard Russo, 2002 (the story of a down-and-out mill town); and *Gilead* by Marilynne Robinson, 2005 (a novel about a minister who looks back on his life).

FUN FACT

Newspaper magnate Joseph Pulitzer created the Pulitzer Prize, "honoring excellence in journalism and the arts since 1917." Ironically, he is also credited—along with William Randolph Hearst—with creating "yellow journalism," a sensationalistic style that was designed to sell newspapers without regard to factual truth.

❑ 272. Write a children's book, even if it's just for your own children or grandchildren.

One of the greatest gifts you can give to a child is an original, imaginative story. For inspiration, turn to your own childhood and life experiences. But don't moralize, at least not overtly—kids hate that.

If you're unsure how to get started, read some of the more popular writers of children's literature, such as Dr. Seuss or Syd Hoff. For an older child, take a page from one of the classics, such as *Alice in Wonderland* or *Charlotte's Web.* And to make the project even more special, create your own unique illustrations.

■ ■ ■ ■

"Books are humanity in print."

—Barbara Tuchman

■ ■ ■ ■

❑ 273. Compose a song.

If you've ever had the urge to be a songwriter, why not give it a whirl? The best place to start is with the lyrics. Choose a topic and write down everything you can think of that relates to it. Now choose a sentence or phrase that sums up what you want to say. That will be your "hook"—often the title of the song. Choose a few more good lines, and try to find rhymes for the ending words in them. Try to go beyond "love" and "dove." Rhymes don't have to be exact—

for example, "pretender" is a fine rhyme for "remember," as is "hour" for "power."

Now arrange your rhymed lines in a pattern. In a typical group of four lines, you could rhyme one with three and two with four, or one with two and three with four, or all four together. Whatever you do, try to be consistent from verse to verse.

Now for the tune. Most songs follow a pattern, where A, B, and C are musical phrases: AB-AB-C-AB or perhaps AAAB-AAAC. If you don't have any musical ability, pick an old tune, and write a new lyric for it. It also helps to study your favorite songs to see how they are structured.

■ ■ ■ ■

"Songwriting starts by being a very internally motivated thing, a personal form of expression that needs to happen for a personal reason, and you don't have a sense of it being received by anyone."

—James Taylor

■ ■ ■ ■

❏ 274. Learn how to play "Chopsticks" on the piano.

You can hear it in your mind, can't you? Did you know that it's actually a waltz? Since 1877, when a 16-year-old British girl first composed it, "The Celebrated Chop Waltz" has become a part of worldwide culture. Euphemia Allen wrote the song under the pseudonym "Arthur de Lulli" and composed it with arrangements for both solo and duet. It's not difficult to learn, and if you ask around a little at your next friend or family get-together, you're likely to find someone who can teach you how to play it. Try the duet with your teacher, once you have it down.

❑ 275. Learn to play the bagpipes.

If you've been hankering to learn a new musical instrument, consider the bagpipes. You don't have to be Scottish to play (nor do you have to wear a kilt), but you do have to have nimble fingers and strong lungs.

A Bagpipe Mystery

How the bagpipes came to Scotland remains a mystery. Some historians believe the instrument was developed there, while others maintain it was either a Roman or Irish import. Regardless, the Scottish Highlanders managed to make it their own.

❑ 276. Learn to play the harmonica.

If you've always wanted to play a musical instrument but thought you didn't have any talent, here's good news. Most harmonicas are made to play in a single key—that is, they *only* contain the notes in that key. So if you have a harmonica tuned to the key of C, it's easy to play along with someone playing a song in C. It may take you awhile to pick out a particular melody, but when you're improvising, you can't play a wrong note because that off note isn't there! Also, harmonicas are small, and you can easily find a private place to practice until you feel more confident.

❑ 277. See the Rockettes.

If you're in New York City over the Christmas holidays, enjoy the Radio City Christmas Spectacular, featuring the legendary Rockettes. The high-kicking dancers have been dazzling audiences for more than 75 years.

❑ 278. Attend a concert at Carnegie Hall.

What's the best way to get to Carnegie Hall? Practice! Or buy a ticket to an upcoming performance, which is probably easier.

Carnegie Hall is one of the most famous entertainment venues in New York City. Founded by industrialist Andrew Carnegie, it opened on May 5, 1891, with a concert featur-

ing the United States debut of
Pyotr Tchaikovsky. Since then,
countless performers have
graced its stage, including
Louis Armstrong, the Beatles,
Frank Sinatra, and Luciano
Pavarotti.

For a current calendar,
visit www.carnegiehall.org.

> **FUN FACT**
>
> Carnegie Hall almost faced the wrecking ball in 1960. Luckily, special legislation allowed New York City to purchase the hall for $5 million.

☐ 279. Attend the Boston Pops.

On July 11, 1885, Bostonians enjoyed the first performance of "concerts of a lighter kind of music," as Henry
Lee Higginson put it. Higginson, founder of the Boston
Symphony Orchestra, wanted to provide the public with
appealing music and opportunities to socialize—not to
mention to provide work for musicians during the off-
season. Thus was born the Boston Pops, the most-recorded
orchestra in the world and considered by many to be
"America's Orchestra."
A series of conductors
have led the Pops, most
notably Arthur Fiedler,
John Williams, and,
now, Keith Lockhart.
In recent years, Lock-
hart has brought a
young, creative, and
whimsical approach to
the beloved orchestra
with such programs

> **FUN FACT**
>
> According to the *Guinness Book of World Records*, the Boston Pops holds the record for the largest audience ever to attend an orchestra concert, a record it set on July 4, 1976, with 400,000 people in attendance. The Pops later broke their own record—in 1998, 2003, and 2004.

as "A Tribute to Oscar and Tony," featuring movie and show tunes and collaborations with the likes of Elvis Costello and Steven Tyler (of Aerosmith), as well as the usual beloved 4th of July and Christmas concerts.

The Boston Pops usually perform at Symphony Hall in Boston—one of the top symphonic halls in the world—but you can also catch them at free summer concerts at the Esplanade along the Charles River in Boston, at occasional appearances around New England, and at their summer concerts at Tanglewood in Stockbridge, Massachusetts.

❏ *280. Visit the Grand Ole Opry.*

The Grand Ole Opry is the Mecca for country music fans. Since country music is a quintessential American art form and a defining note in our musical culture, it's worth a visit even if you can't stand the twang of a steel guitar. And, it's in Nashville, which—no matter how you look at it—is a pretty cool town.

The Opry began as a radio show in 1925, just five years after the new medium of radio was born. Not too many years later, the radio signal was boosted enough so that most listeners in the United States and parts of Canada could tune in if they wanted. Today, the Grand Ole Opry is a performance venue and a television show and has nearly a cult following. The original stage was the Ryman Auditorium, which is back in use today after a period of decline. Built as a church in 1892, the Ryman Auditorium is a National Historic Landmark and housed the Grand Ole Opry from 1943–1974. The Opry is now staged in a newer, larger venue built in the 1970s.

281. Take a stroll down Beale Street at night.

Beale Street in downtown Memphis is world famous because it is the home of the Blues, and if you have ever walked down this street in the late evening, you will know why. People play their instruments not only in the bars but also all along the street, and the music they play is truly captivating.

The Beale Street Music Festival, held each May, has grown into one of the largest festivals in the United States, drawing people from all over the world to celebrate the birth of the distinctive American music known as the Blues.

FUN FACT

In 1841, entrepreneur and developer Robertson Topp created Beale Street, but it wasn't until two decades later that traveling African American musicians started playing their music on this street.

282. Visit Graceland, the home of Elvis.

If you're a fan of Elvis Presley and you haven't been to Graceland in Memphis, Tennessee, you owe it to yourself to make that sojourn. Even if you're not a fan, touring his estate, the Elvis Presley Car Museum, and the Elvis in Hollywood Exhibit is a cultural experience you shouldn't pass up. Elvis is considered one of the most important icons of 20th-century America.

❏ 283. Visit the Rock and Roll Hall of Fame and Museum in Cleveland.

Join the 500,000 people who come each year to "the house that rock built" on the shores of Lake Erie in Cleveland, Ohio. As varied and creative as rock itself, the Rock and Roll Hall of Fame and Museum features exhibits that focus on the roots of rock and roll, the pioneering early artists, soul music, the evolution of audio technology, and today's new artists.

Among the museum's priceless artifacts are the original band uniforms worn by the Beatles on the Sgt. Pepper album cover; the lyrics to Purple Haze as handwritten by Jimi Hendrix; guitars owned by Les Paul, Duane Allman, and others; Buddy Holly's high school diploma; and much more. There's even a recreation of Sun Studios

> ## The First Performers to be Inducted into the Rock and Roll Hall of Fame in 1986
>
> Chuck Berry, James Brown, Ray Charles, Sam Cooke, Antoine "Fats" Domino, Don Everly, Phil Everly, Buddy Holly, Jerry Lee Lewis, "Little" Richard Penniman, and Elvis Presley.

that includes the original equipment on which Elvis Presley, Jerry Lee Lewis, and others recorded their first hits.

Each year, new members are inducted into the museum's Hall of Fame, with a multi-media gallery that features three giant screens, telling the story of the Rock and Roll Hall of Fame inductees.

If you're a real rock and roll fan, plan to spend a couple of days looking at all the exhibits, listening to the interactive displays, and watching the video—there are more than five hours of film alone!

❑ 284. Attend an opera.

Give your life some class by attending an opera. You will marvel at the music, the scenery, the costumes, and the story—even if it's not in English.

FUN FACT

Operas were first performed in Italy at the end of the 16th century.

❑ 285. Visit the Butchart Gardens on Vancouver Island, B.C.

It's a story of transformation: an unsightly mining pit, painstakingly top-soiled and tended into an Eden-esque landscape. Cement producer Robert Pim Butchart had exhausted the resources of his lime quarry in the early 1900s. The dug-up land, located near the Butchart home, somehow inspired Butchart's wife, Jennie, to begin a gardening project. She had soil brought in by horse-drawn carts from surrounding farms, and thus began her work of art. The incredible Sunken Garden would be just the beginning of the wonders yet to come.

Today, in addition to Jennie Butchart's first gardening feat, the grounds boast a Japanese Garden, Italian Garden, Rose Garden, and Begonia Bower, along with fountains and water features, art sculptures, and other attractions. The Butchart Gardens is still a family business; they've gained an international reputation and are recognized as a premier West Coast display garden. Fifty gardeners use more than

1,000,000 bedding plants in some 700 varieties throughout the gardens each year for uninterrupted blossoming from March through October. Although the annual number of visitors approaches one million, be assured that there is plenty of room within the acres of loveliness to find and feel solitude and tranquility during your visit to this treasure of British Columbia.

■ ■ ■ ■

"The greatest gift of the garden is the restoration of the five senses."

—Hanna (Mrs. Alpheus B. Hervey) Rion

■ ■ ■ ■

❏ 286. Drive from Banff to Jasper in Alberta, Canada.

National Geographic begins its praise of this route by stating, "Starting on the fringe of the Great Plains and climbing through the incomparable mountain scenery of Banff and Jasper National Parks, this magnificent drive—one of the crown jewels of western Canada—combines exhilarating vistas of forest, crag, and glacier."

When you take this memorable drive, slow down, take your time, and savor this powerful encounter with the Canadian wilderness. Its natural beauty will make your heart ache and provides the thrill of rugged wilderness replete with elk, bighorn sheep, and bear, as well as lots of accessible trails for experiencing and viewing the variety of terrain on this route. Mountains, rivers, hot springs, fjord-like lakes, canyons, glaciers, waterfalls, museums, and a tramway in Jasper from which to get a bird's-eye view are all along the way through this virtual paradise on earth.

You'll want to plan this trip sometime between the months of June and September, and for accommodations or campsites, it's best to make reservations. Visitors naturally gather at the more popular sites, so if you're not fond of crowds, plan to get to these attractions before 10 A.M. or in the early evening.

❑ *287. Attend a performance of Cirque du Soleil.*

There are circuses and then there's Cirque du Soleil, an awe-inspiring blend of music, art, and agility guaranteed to bring out your inner child. Founded in Montreal in 1984, Cirque du Soleil currently produces more than a dozen shows throughout the world. Las Vegas is home to several productions, including Mystère, "O," Zumanity, "Kà," and The Beatles-Love. Cirque du Soleil shows also tour most major cities.

Cirque du Soleil incorporates a variety of elements, including acrobatics, dance, and pyrotechnics, and each production revolves around a central theme. Give it a try—you'll come home amazed.

"Time is a circus, always packing up and moving away."

—Ben Hecht

❏ 288. Visit the Alps in Europe.

Several European countries play host to this mythic mountain range, which is one of the world's great wonders. Among these nations are Austria and Slovenia in the east, through Germany, Liechtenstein, Switzerland, and Italy, and then France in the west. On the Italian–French border is Mont Blanc, the highest mountain in the Alps.

■ ■ ■ ■

"Today is your day! Your mountain is waiting. So . . . get on your way."
—Dr. Seuss, from *Oh, the Places You'll Go!*

■ ■ ■ ■

❏ 289. Tour the castles of Europe.

The United States is a great country, but it doesn't have nearly enough castles. To really enjoy these wonderful fortified residences, take a trip to Europe. Indeed, Europe is the world's castle king. No matter which country you visit— England, Scotland, Ireland, France, Germany, Switzerland, Italy, Czech Republic, Austria, Spain—you'll find a wide variety of colorful castles open to the public.

In fact, castles have become such a popular destination that many companies now offer international excursions that focus on nothing else. Every day, for one week or two, you get to visit one castle after another while a guide tells you about the history of each. Such tours are never boring, however, because each castle is unique in design and architecture, and castle styles vary from country to country and region to region.

290. Attend the Vienna Philharmonic.

Classical music enthusiasts have a lot of venues at which to enjoy their favorite melodies. But for a truly special experience, attend a concert by the Vienna Philharmonic in Austria. Few other orchestras are as closely associated with European classical music as the Vienna Philharmonic. Over its 160-plus years, the orchestra has performed the best-known music from all of the best-known classical composers. In fact, no less an authority than Richard Wagner called the Vienna Philharmonic one of the most outstanding orchestras in the world, a sentiment echoed by nearly all of his contemporaries.

■ ■ ■ ■

"All praise of the Vienna Philharmonic reveals itself as understatement."

—Richard Strauss

■ ■ ■ ■

291. Attend the Salzburg Marionette Theatre in Salzburg, Austria.

This is no ordinary puppet show! The Salzburg Marionette Theatre enjoys a world-class reputation for its performance of classical operas, operettas, ballets, and more recently, even some plays. The theater's "high-strung" performers enact these with such skill and precision as to provide the illusion that the marionettes have come to life as miniature versions of humanity.

Although the Salzburg Marionette Theatre was established in 1913, the lovely 350-seat baroque theater (in which performances are now held) did not become its home until 1998. As one of the oldest continuing marionette theaters in the world, it's not surprising that its original productions made use of live actors and musicians to provide voices and musical accompaniment for the marionettes' performances. In the 1950s, however, the first recordings were made and helped simplify productions. Today, soundtracks are recorded to provide these features for the company's ever widening repertoire.

If you're tempted to pass this attraction by because it seems like it's more of a "kid thing," you'll thank yourself a million times over for resisting that temptation and treating yourself to an attraction that has entertained military troops, mesmerized adult audiences around the globe, and enchanted even the most skeptical grown-up visitors to Salzburg for nearly 100 years.

■ ■ ■ ■

"There are many advantages in puppets.
They never argue. They have no crude
views about art. They have no private lives."

—Oscar Wilde

■ ■ ■ ■

❑ 292. Drink beer at Oktoberfest in Munich.

The Oktoberfest in Munich is the beer party to end all beer parties—an idea that may not necessarily appeal to you. But this is something you do to say you did it. Oktoberfest is a two-week festival celebrating Germany's beer heritage. It's also the largest beer festival in the world. To partake properly, reserve a seat in one of the many massive beer tents. You'll be drinking with thousands of others. To get a good seat without a reservation, go in the morning.

> **FUN FACT**
>
> The oldest known recorded recipe is for beer, dating 4,000 years ago from the Mesopotamian culture.

❑ 293. Drive the Autobahn.

Germany's Autobahn is arguably the most famous highway in the world, a stretch of asphalt where speed limits are scoffed at and slow drivers are left in the dust. Are you man or woman enough to live life in the fast lane? There's only one way to find out.

The Autobahn is not a single highway, but a series of roadways built throughout Germany. The first were constructed in the 1930s and 1940s, and today there are more than 7,500 miles of limited access, high-speed roads.

Driving the Autobahn is an amazing experience. If you have the opportunity, rent a car and give it a test drive. You'll never forget it!

❑ 294. See the tulips in Holland.

The tulip is one of the most recognizable symbols of Holland and the perfect reason to visit this beautiful European country. Thousands of tourists annually visit Holland just to marvel at the colorful tulip fields and participate in various flower festivals. The season begins in March with crocuses, followed by daffodils and yellow narcissi.

> **FUN FACT**
>
> Holland, Michigan, displays not only countless tulips every spring but also an authentic Dutch windmill, which was transported there from Holland. Visit this American town if you can't go across the Atlantic.

Hyacinths and tulips start to bloom in May, and the gladioli burst forth in August.

Flower parades are common throughout Holland from April to September. The largest is the Bollenstreek Flower Parade, which is held at the end of April.

❑ 295. Visit the Anne Frank House.

One of the most touching and tragic stories to emerge from World War II was the story of Anne Frank, a young Jewish girl who kept a diary of the struggles she and her family experienced while hiding from the Nazis. Honor Anne's memory by visiting the Anne Frank House and Museum in Amsterdam.

In July 1942, the Frank family went into hiding in back of the house that now bears Anne's name to escape escalating Nazi persecution against Jews in the Netherlands. They were later joined by four others. The group managed to remain undetected for two years, but were ultimately betrayed and deported. Anne and her sister, Margot, died of typhus in the Bergen-Belsen concentration camp in March 1945, just weeks before the Allied forces liberated the camp. Anne's father, Otto, was the only member of the family to survive the war. Anne's diary was returned to him upon his return to the Netherlands. In 1947, her diary was published in the Netherlands and has since been translated into 55 languages.

The Anne Frank House, located at Prinsengracht 263, is a moving tribute to the bravery and fortitude of a family facing overwhelming adversity, as well as that of all who were persecuted by the Nazis during World War II. It is not to be missed.

❑ 296. Visit the Louvre and view the Mona Lisa.

The Louvre in Paris, France, is without question the world's most famous museum, and its prize attraction is Leonardo Da Vinci's *Mona Lisa,* the world's best-known painting. To go your entire life without seeing this remarkable work in person would be a shame.

Expect a crowd, however, when you go. Despite the fact that the Louvre is home to 35,000 works of art, including the Venus de Milo, it's the *Mona Lisa*—also known as *La Gioconda*—that draws the most people. But an up-close viewing is well worth the wait.

So who was this enigmatic model renowned throughout the world? Her name was Lisa Gherardini del Giocondo, and she was the wife of a Florentine cloth merchant. According to experts, Da Vinci started her portrait between 1503 and 1506.

Tracking the Mona Lisa

The *Mona Lisa* has had some incredible adventures over the years. In 1911, this famous painting was stolen from the Salon Carre in the Louvre and recovered three years later. And on December 30, 1956, a Bolivian man named Ugo Ungaza Villegas threw a stone at the painting, damaging a speck of pigment near the image's left elbow. The painting is now roped off and protected behind special glass.

❑ 297. Stroll down the Champs-Élysées in Paris.

One of the most romantic streets in the world is The Avenue des Champs-Élysées, with its famous cafés, shops, and cinemas. Take the person you love most with you to Paris, and walk hand-in-hand with that special person down this enchanting street.

FUN FACT

Champs-Élysées is French for "Elysian Fields," the place of the blessed in Greek mythology.

❑ 298. Visit the Eiffel Tower.

The Eiffel Tower is the tallest structure in Paris, France, which alone makes it worth a visit. Kiss your significant other while standing on the observation deck, and you've got a memory that will last a lifetime.

❑ 299. Climb to the top of the Arc de Triomphe in Paris.

You may be out of breath by the time you reach the top of the Arc de Triomphe, or the "Arc of Triumph," but what a sight you'll see, with the arteries of streets running into the circle, the heart of Paris. It is a monument that honors the French soldiers who have fought for their country, and it is a wondrous sight, especially when it is lit at night.

FUN FACT

There are 284 steps to the top of the Arc, or you can be lazy and take the one lift.

❑ 300. Go on a bateaux-mouches on the Seine and see the Notre Dame Cathedral.

One of the most, if not *the* most, famous Catholic cathedral in the world is Notre Dame de Paris, where many significant events took place, including the wedding of Mary I of Scotland and François II of France in 1558 and the canonization of Joan of Arc in 1920. Its construction began in the 12th century and was completed in the 14th century. See the magnificent architecture of this church, which is regarded as a great example of French Gothic architecture, while riding on an excursion boat on the fabulous Seine River.

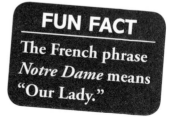

FUN FACT

The French phrase *Notre Dame* means "Our Lady."

❑ 301. Attend a Paris fashion show.

You don't have to be Paris Hilton to attend a Paris fashion show. The fact is, most major fashion shows sell tickets, so pretty much anyone can attend. If you want a front-row seat, however, then you DO have to be Paris Hilton. Or at least someone equally famous.

First, confirm the dates of Fashion Week, which vary from year to year, at www.modeaparis.com. Then contact the shows you want to attend (they are usually divided into spring/summer and fall/winter), and inquire about ticket availability. If you can't make it to Paris, New York and London also host annual fashion events.

■ ■ ■ ■

"Fashions fade, style is eternal."

—Yves Saint Laurent

■ ■ ■ ■

❑ 302. Visit the Palace of Versailles.

Palaces are a dime a dozen in Europe. Every city, it seems, has several of them. None, however, compares to the Palace of Versailles in France. It's one of the most opulent, as well as historic, palaces in Europe, and it's something everyone must experience in person to fully appreciate.

FUN FACT

Building Versailles required nearly 30,000 laborers and was so expensive that it nearly bankrupted the nation.

The Palace of Versailles was the official residence of the kings of France from 1682 to 1789. It was built in 1624 as a hunting lodge for Louis XIII and expanded into a palatial home by his successor, Louis XIV, starting in 1669. The Palace was stripped of most of its furnishings during the French Revolution and is now a national museum.

The Palace and its grounds are quite large, and several companies offer half-day and full-day tours from nearby Paris. Highlights include the Royal Apartments, Hall of Mirrors, Queen's Bedroom, and the Gallery of Battles, which offers an audio guide in eight languages.

You'll need a few hours more to tour the palace gardens and visit the Queen's Hamlet, where Marie Antoinette maintained a flock of sheep. Tours of the Grand Trianon are also available. It's a minipalace where Louis XV and Louis XVI enjoyed relaxing outside the court of Versailles.

❏ *303. Attend the Cannes Film Festival.*

Do you love movies? How about sun-drenched beaches? If both excite you, then go to France next May for the Cannes Film Festival. It's one of the oldest and most influential film festivals in the world, and it's something every film buff should attend at least once.

The Cannes Film Festival debuted in 1946 and very quickly became *the* international event to see and be seen. Directors and producers found it the perfect venue to introduce their latest epics, and stars and starlets could often be seen wandering up and down the resort town's sandy beaches while eager photographers snapped their pictures.

Today, dozens of films are screened during the two-week festival, with 20 films competing for the coveted Palme d'Or, the event's most prestigious award. A variety of short films, as well as movies made by international film-makers, are also presented. In addition, producers often use the festival to find distributors for their latest films or funding for future projects.

If you decide to attend the Cannes Film Festival, plan your trip well in advance. The town's hotels fill quickly, and latecomers often find themselves having to stay many miles away from the events.

❑ 304. Lay on the sands of the French Riviera.

The French Riviera is the name commonly used to describe the *Côte d'Azur,* which lies on the Mediterranean coast-line of the southeastern corner of France, extending from Menton near the Italian border in the east to either Hyères or Cassis in the west. It is a favorite resort for European celebrities. Why don't you join them?

❑ 305. See the cave paintings in France.

The most priceless paintings in the world weren't created by Rembrandt or Da Vinci; they were drawn by men and women living in a cave in Dordogne, France, more than 17,000 years ago. If our early ancestors fascinate you, a trip to the region is a must.

In 1940, four curious teenage boys discovered the Lascaux cave paintings, which are considered one of the most important archaeological finds in modern history. The main cave and several steep galleries are decorated with hundreds of engraved, drawn, and colorfully painted figures of prehistoric animals and symbols. Among the most spectacular are four large aurochs (giant European cattle, now extinct), some measuring 16 feet; there are also red deer, large cats, and bison.

In 1948, the cave system was opened to tourists, resulting in extensive damage to the delicate artwork. In 1964, the caves were closed to the public so experts could correct or reverse the destruction. In 1983, a partial replica of the paintings, known as Lascaux II, was opened to satisfy public curiosity. Lascaux II reproduces nearly 200 paintings and shows visitors what the closed-off cave looks like inside.

❑ 306. Take a trip on the Orient Express.

The Venice Simplon-Orient Express, popularly known as the Orient Express, is one of the most famous trains in the world. It has a remarkable history, including being the setting for one of Agatha Christie's most well-known murder mysteries. Before you kick the bucket, take a journey aboard this magnificent line.

The Venice Simplon-Orient Express takes passengers to some of the greatest cities in Europe, including London, Paris, Venice, Budapest, Prague, Krakow, and Istanbul. As you make your way across the continent, you'll pass breathtaking mountains, racing rivers, gorgeous lakes, quaint villages, and bustling cities. And you'll do it all in luxury, while enjoying meals prepared by top chefs. And if you're wondering how it travels across the English Channel, passengers are conveyed from and to England and the continent by coach on the Eurotunnel shuttle through the Channel Tunnel.

For further information about the Orient Express, visit www.orient-express.com. For itineraries and booking details, consult your travel agent.

Some Express History

The Orient Express has had a colorful history. For example, King Boris III of Bulgaria was a regular passenger who enjoyed driving the train whenever he was aboard. And in 1929, the train became stuck in heavy snow 60 miles outside Istanbul for several days. Passengers survived with the assistance of nearby Turkish villagers. The Orient Express also served in World War II, with both the German Army and the U.S. Transportation Corps employing it.

❑ 307. Take the Chunnel from England to France.

The Channel Tunnel, which travels under the English Channel to connect England with France, is one of the world's most astounding feats of modern engineering. Hop on for the ride of your life!

Known colloquially as the "Chunnel," the Channel Tunnel speeds travelers from London to Paris (or vice versa) in just 2 hours and 15 minutes via high-speed train. The Chunnel contains three tracks. The outer two are for passenger trains, and the smaller inner track is for a guidance shuttle train.

If you have to travel between England and France, the Chunnel allows you to make the trip in comfort.

And the Winner Is...

The Channel Tunnel took seven years to construct at a cost of $21 billion and required 15,000 workers. England and France had a friendly competition to see who could reach the middle first (England won by a nose). Construction was completed in 1994.

❑ 308. Witness the Changing of the Guard at Buckingham Palace.

The Changing of the Guard at Buckingham Palace is one of the most popular attractions among London visitors. Hundreds of people line up to witness the event daily, and you should try to see it as well.

    The Changing of the Guard takes place in the forecourt of Buckingham Palace at 11 A.M. There is much pomp and pageantry while the Military Band performs for the assembled crowd. If you decide to attend, arrive early so you'll get a good viewing spot. Because the Changing of the Guard is popular among tourists, it tends to get a bit crowded.

FUN FACT

The building that forms the core of Buckingham Palace was originally a townhouse built for the Duke of Buckingham in 1703.

❑ 309. See Big Ben.

One of the most famous timepieces in the world is Big Ben, the amazingly reliable four-faced clock that towers over downtown London. If you ever need to set your watch, it's the place to turn.

Arguably England's most recognizable landmark, Big Ben adjoins the Palace of Westminster, where Parliament meets, and became operational on September 7, 1859. Its name refers not to the clock tower but to the 13-ton bell that hangs within, named after Benjamin Hall, London's first commissioner of works.

❑ 310. Attend a service at Westminster Abbey.

Westminster Abbey is one of the most famous churches in the world, so the next time you're in London, plan to attend a service. The present church, which Henry III started in 1245, holds daily services, which include prayer and Holy Communion. It also conducts special services on religious holidays. In addition

to being a house of worship, Westminster Abbey contains more than 1,000 years of history, including a wealth of paintings, stained glass, pavements, textiles, and other works of art.

❑ 311. Visit Oxford and Cambridge universities.

Two of the world's most distinguished institutions of higher learning are the University of Oxford and the University of Cambridge. You don't have to be a student to enjoy their history and tradition, so the next time you're in England, drop by for a visit.

Oxford is the oldest university in the English-speaking world. Its beginnings can be traced back to the end of the 11th century, though the exact date of its founding is uncertain. Cambridge was founded shortly after a handful of academics fled Oxford in 1209 following a run-in with local residents. As a result, the two universities have enjoyed a friendly rivalry for centuries. They are both located in towns with the same names.

Rhodes Scholars

The Rhodes Scholarships are the world's oldest international fellowships. They were named for benefactor Cecil Rhodes, who died in 1902, and bring exceptional students from around the world to the University of Oxford for extra study. The first American recipients entered Oxford in 1904.

❑ 312. Take a photo of yourself crossing Abbey Road.

One of the most iconic images of the Beatles is a photo of "The Fab Four" crossing Abbey Road for the album cover of the same name. The next time you're in London with friends, take a picture of yourselves recreating that famous photo shot.

313. Enjoy a traditional afternoon tea in England.

The British are big on tradition, and one of their most popular customs is afternoon tea. Even if you're not British, it's still a pleasure to enjoy this little bit of civility. The afternoon tea became fashionable among England's high society during the 1880s, when men and women would dress up for a bit of socializing around 4 P.M. The event generally includes hot tea served in delicate bone china, small sandwiches, pastries, and preserves. Women traditionally wear gowns and gloves, and men wear dress clothes.

> **FUN FACT**
>
> In 1840, Anna, the seventh Duchess of Bedford, introduced the afternoon tea as a way to sate her afternoon hunger.

314. Visit Madame Tussauds Wax Museum.

There are numerous wax museums around the world, but none compare to Madame Tussauds. It's the gold standard for celebrity likenesses, and the museum is something that can be appreciated only in person.

Madame Tussauds has been in business for more than 200 years, and it currently has museums in London, Amsterdam, Berlin, Hong

> **FUN FACT**
>
> During the French Revolution, Madame Tussaud was forced to prove her allegiance to the cause by casting death masks of executed aristocrats.

Kong, Shanghai, New York, Las Vegas, Hollywood, and Washington, D.C. Each museum is unique and chock full of famous actors, politicians, and sports figures. At the London museum, some of Madame Tussaud's earliest works are still on display.

Madame Tussauds may be your only opportunity to get up close and personal with some of the world's best-known celebrities, so make sure you don't pass it up.

❑ *315. Visit Stonehenge.*

Stonehenge is located in Wilshire County, England, and is one of Britain's most popular tourist attractions. It is something everyone must see up close to appreciate. Much more than just a circle of big stone slabs, Stonehenge represents the awe and mystery of Britain's amazing past.

The first stage of Stonehenge is believed to have been constructed approximately 5,000 years ago, and the stones erected many years later. Who built Stonehenge and why remains unknown, but considering the mind-boggling amount of work that went into its construction, it must have been extremely important to those who built it.

> ## Stonehenge Stones
> The huge stones that form Stonehenge's outer ring weigh as much as 50 tons each. It is estimated that more than 1,000 men were needed to maneuver the stones past the steepest parts of the 20-mile route from Marlborough Downs.

Today Stonehenge is a far cry from what it used to be. Over time, several slabs were taken for use in home and road construction, and damage to some of the smaller stones has resulted in a prohibition of human contact. In other words, you can look but don't touch.

The next time you're in England, book a tour to Stonehenge. It's a prehistoric marvel of engineering that you'll never forget.

❑ *316. Kiss the Blarney Stone.*

Feeling a little tongue-tied lately? Plan a vacation to Ireland so you can kiss the Blarney Stone. According to legend, anyone who kisses the magical rock will become a more eloquent speaker.

The Blarney Castle is located in the village of Blarney, about five miles northwest of Cork. The castle was built in 1446 and is an impressive 90 feet tall. It's one of

> **FUN FACT**
> The word "blarney" is now a part of the English lexicon and means clever, flattering, or persuasive speech.

Ireland's most popular tourist attractions, drawing more than 300,000 visitors a year, and excursions to the castle are plentiful.

The Blarney Stone is steeped in legend. One myth suggests that it's the rock that Moses struck to produce water for the Israelites during their exodus from Egypt. Another states that it's the stone that David hid behind while fleeing from King Saul and was brought to Ireland during the Crusades.

Kissing the Blarney Stone is no easy feat; you have to bend over backward—literally. At one time, smoochers were hung by their heels over the edge of the parapet, but that practice stopped when one pilgrim slipped from his friends' grasp and plunged to his death. Today, visitors sit with their backs to the stone and lean backward while someone firmly holds their legs.

❑ 317. See the Rock of Gibraltar.

If you want to see the only wild primates (Barbary Macaques) in Europe, then you have to visit this famous monolithic promontory. Tourists also enjoy walking through the many tunnels within the Rock,

FUN FACT

The Rock of Gibraltar was one of the Pillars of Hercules. According to Greek mythology, Hercules smashed a mountain in two to connect the Atlantic Ocean and the Mediterranean Sea to form the Strait of Gibraltar. One part of the mountain became the Rock of Gibraltar.

which is the property of the United Kingdom and located off the southwestern tip of Europe on the Iberian Peninsula.

❑ 318. Visit the Parthenon in Athens.

FUN FACT

The Parthenon was a Greek temple dedicated to the Greek goddess, Athena.

Ancient Athens was the cradle of Western civilization. Literature, philosophy, medicine, mathematics, even government in the West can find its roots in Athens, and the center of activity was the Acropolis, which was called the "Sacred Rock" of Athens. Between 447 and 438 B.C., its most famous monument was built—the Parthenon. Make travel plans today to see it in the near future.

❑ 319. Visit the Colosseum.

Of all the sites to see in Rome, the Colosseum is surely the most amazing. Picture a sports arena that held 50,000 people—from the wealthy folks in the lower box seats to the rabble up in the nosebleed section; with 80 entrances so patrons could get in and out quickly; where gladiators fought against wild beasts and each other; where the floors could be flooded so miniature sea battles could be reenacted; where martyrs met their deaths. Now imagine standing where it all happened almost 2,000 years ago.

❑ 320. Visit the Sistine Chapel.

One of the best-known sites within Vatican City is the Sistine Chapel, which is located in the Apostolic Palace— the Pope's official residence and the site of papal elections. Even if you're not Catholic, its awe-inspiring beauty demands an in-person visit.

One of the highlights of the Sistine Chapel is the 12,000-square-foot painting on its ceiling created by Michelangelo between 1508 and 1512. Michelangelo, however, was only one of several Renaissance artists to add to the chapel's pageantry. Others include Raphael, Bernini, and Botticelli.

The Sistine Chapel is named after Pope Sixtus IV, who commissioned its construction in 1475. In 1481, Sixtus IV summoned Botticelli, Domenico Ghirlandaio, Cosimo Rosselli, and others to decorate the walls with frescoes. Unlike Michelangelo's years-long work on the ceiling, the fresco project took only 11 months, from July 1481 to May 1482. It was consecrated and dedicated to the Assumption of the Virgin on August 15, 1483.

> **"Without having seen the Sistine Chapel one can form no appreciable idea of what one man is capable of achieving."**
> —Johann Wolfgang Goethe

❑ *321. Attend Mass by the Pope.*

For a remarkable religious experience, attend Mass given by the pope, whether in Vatican City or elsewhere. You don't have to be Catholic to find spiritual solace in the service—the Holy Father's message is universal for many. Expect crowds; millions revere the pope.

FUN FACT

The current pope, Benedict XVI, is the 265th pope of Rome.

❑ *322. Ride a gondola in Venice.*

Venice, Italy, is famous for many attractions, such as its watery streets and its picturesque gondolas. No trip to the City of Canals would be complete without taking a romantic ride in one of these historic boats.

Gondola rides are a popular tourist activity in Venice, and numerous boats with eager gondoliers can be found throughout the main tourist areas. A night ride will cost you more, as will a ride with a singing gondolier.

The Traghetto

If you'd like a quick gondola ride without having to pay big bucks, try a public gondola ferry, known as the traghetto. These boats take you across the main Grand Canal at about a half dozen points between the railroad station and St. Mark's Square.

❑ 323. See the Leaning Tower of Pisa.

If you're ever in Italy, you must see this intriguing structure. Begun in 1174, the famed tower began leaning before it was even completed. Today, you can walk the 294 steps for great views of

Galileo's Weighty Experiment

Legend says it was at the Tower of Pisa that Galileo dropped two balls of different weights to prove that they would reach the ground at the same time. Unfortunately, historians believe it's just a legend, first told by Galileo's secretary and biographer, who may have been trying to build up his master's reputation.

the city of Pisa. Just don't look down!

❑ 324. Backpack across Europe.

As a teenager, did you ever dream of putting all your worries on hold and backpacking across Europe? It's not too late to make that special dream come true.

Obviously, backpacking across Europe requires some planning and isn't something you should do on the spur of the moment. For safety and companionship, get a friend or relative to accompany you. Then set an itinerary, including the countries you plan to visit, how long you'll be staying in each, and when you expect to return home.

Money can be saved on hotels by staying at less expensive youth hostels, which are common throughout Europe. But even if you do that, an extended excursion across Europe will still be expensive, so plan accordingly. A combination of cash, which can be exchanged for euros or local currency, and a credit card should get you through the trip. A cell phone with an international calling plan will help you stay in touch with folks back home, but carry an international phone card with you in case of emergency. And don't forget your passport.

❑ 325. See the fjords of Norway.

FUN FACT

Glacial activity formed the fjords of Norway during the ice age about 20,000 years ago.

Among nature's most spectacular landscapes are the fjords in Norway. A trip to Scandinavia is not complete unless you view one of the four western fjord regions of Norway with its awesome mountains, lakes, rivers, and forests.

☐ 326. Visit the Viking Ship Museum in Oslo, Norway.

This museum is part of the Museum of Cultural History of the University of Oslo. Its archaeological exhibits include ships, sledges, wood carvings, jewelry, and other artifacts from the Viking Age (8th to 11th centuries). The three ships on display are the best-preserved Viking ships known, and they provide an unforgettable image of the fascinating world of the Vikings.

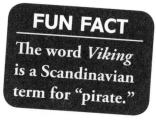

FUN FACT

The word *Viking* is a Scandinavian term for "pirate."

☐ 327. Visit Red Square in Moscow.

This important city hub is the starting point of several main streets that become major highways outside the city and extend throughout all of Russia. It is arguably one of the most famous city squares in the world. Throughout its rich history, Red Square has maintained an ongoing political and cultural significance in Russia.

Sights you'll want to see when you're there include Lenin's Tomb and Nikolskaya Tower, the State Historical Museum, GUM

FUN FACT

The "Red" in Red Square refers neither to the color of the city's bricks nor to the color red used by the Communist Party. It's actually from the Russian word *krasnaya*, which means "red" or "beautiful." But that meaning has now become archaic, so Red Square it is!

department store, St. Basil's Cathedral, the palaces and cathedrals of the Kremlin, the Kazan Cathedral, and the Iberian Gate and chapel.

❑ 328. Take a boat ride on the Caspian Sea.

What is the largest freshwater lake in the world? In terms of surface area, it is the Caspian Sea, which is enclosed by Russia, Iran, Kazakhstan, Turkmenistan, and Azerbaijan. It has a surface area of 143,244 square miles. So when you are in a boat in the middle of it, you feel as though you are in the middle of an ocean. On your next vacation, experience that feeling, and maybe go fishing there as well.

> **FUN FACT**
>
> In terms of volume of water, Lake Baikal in southern Siberia, Russia, is the world's largest freshwater lake. It is also the deepest lake. Lake Baikal contains about 5,521 cubic miles of water or approximately 20 percent of Earth's fresh surface water. Now that's a lot of water.

❑ 329. Stand on Masada in Israel.

The word *Masada* is derived from a Hebrew word meaning "fortress." It's an apt name for this high, isolated plateau that has historically served as a location for hunkering down to fend off foes. Jews and Romans alike used it for this purpose. The cliffs on the east edge are a dizzying 1,300 feet high, while the western cliffs are a "mere" 300 feet. The top is flat, and its dimensions are approximately 1,800 feet by 900 feet. While you can ascend to the top by the Snake Path on the eastern side or the Roman ramp on the west side, a cable car is also at hand to take the strain out of getting to the top if you wish to avail yourself of it.

❑ *330. See the Dead Sea Scrolls.*

In 1947, a young shepherd in search of a wandering goat tossed a rock into a cave and heard, instead of a bleat, the crack of a ceramic pot. The rest is history—ancient history, since the pot and others like it contained scrolls that were 2,000 years old. The Dead Sea Scrolls, as they came to be called, comprise fragments from 850 different documents and include the oldest evidence for biblical texts in the world. Chief among them is the Great Isaiah Scroll, which dates from around 100 B.C. and is the oldest known copy of the Book of Isaiah in existence.

Where can you see these fascinating ancient documents? Although portions of them are occasionally loaned to other museums for special exhibitions, the best place to see them is at the Shrine of the Book, a wing of the Israel Museum in Jerusalem specially constructed to house the scrolls.

❑ *331. Visit the Wailing Wall in Jerusalem.*

The Western Wall, also known as the Wailing Wall, is one of the most revered sites in the Jewish religion. It bears a fascinating history and should be a stop for everyone visiting Israel. Located in the Old City of Jerusalem, the Wall is the section of the western supporting wall of the Temple Mount and has remained intact since the destruction of the Second Jerusalem Temple in A.D. 70.

Devout Jews frequently gather at the Wall to offer prayers to God, and it's common to see men and women standing before it, heads bowed, silently expressing gratitude or praying for divine mercy. It is also common practice to place slips of paper containing written prayers or requests into the Wall's crevices, an act that dates back hundreds of years.

Although the Western Wall is often crowded, it's relatively easy to get to by both bus and car. When you go, remember that the Wall is a holy place and be respectful of those around you.

❏ *332. See the Sea of Galilee.*

The Sea of Galilee is Israel's largest freshwater lake, and it is where Jesus of Nazareth's ministry took place. Take a boat across this lake, and observe the waters that Jesus and his closest disciples were on when a storm nearly sank their boat. Also observe the many beautiful flowers that line the shores and the abundant fish that are caught daily. It is a fascinating experience for the religious and nonreligious alike.

The Jesus Boat

In 1986, two brothers, Moshe and Yuval Lufan, discovered the remains of an ancient fishing boat from the first century A.D. Although this boat is called "The Jesus Boat," there is no evidence that Jesus and his followers were connected to it. Nevertheless, it does give us an idea of what kind of boat Jesus was in. "The Jesus Boat," or "Sea of Galilee Boat," is housed in the Yigal Alon Museum in Kibbutz Ginosar.

333. Visit the pyramids in Giza, Egypt.

Only one of the Seven Wonders of the Ancient World still stands: the Great Pyramid of Giza. For nearly 4,000 years, it was the largest man-made structure in the world.

There are actually three pyramids in the region: the Great Pyramid of Khufu, the Pyramid of Kafhre, and the Pyramid of Menkaura. Each is a tomb dedicated to a different king.

The largest of the three, the Great Pyramid of Khufu, is a massive monument, with a base that covers nearly 13 acres. It is believed to have taken 20 years to construct and was completed around 2560 B.C.

334. See the Great Sphinx of Giza.

Along with the Great Pyramid, the Sphinx is a must-see for anyone visiting Egypt. The date of its construction is unknown, but the monument's head is believed to be the pharaoh Khafra. The rest of the body is depicted as a lion in a reclined position.

335. Visit the Sahara desert.

The Sahara desert is one of the largest and best-known deserts in the world. Be the envy of all of your friends by visiting this stunning sea of sand on your next vacation.

You don't have to be Lawrence of Arabia to make this happen. A variety of companies throughout West Africa, including Egypt, Morocco, and Mali, offer multiday excursions that allow you to travel this unique vista via camel, just as the Bedouins have done for hundreds of years. (If you're not a camel person, truck caravans are also available.) Everything is provided, including food and shelter for those days when you will be camping under the gorgeous desert sky. Water is collected from desert wells. It's drinkable, but it is advised that you bring purification tablets, just to be safe.

Deserts Worldwide

Approximately one-third of the Earth's land surface is covered by desert, and North America is no stranger to these extreme environments. In fact, it's home to four major desert regions: Chihuahuan, Sonoran, Mojave, and Great Basin.

Keep in mind that desert temperatures can reach a blistering 120 degrees F. Most caravans take a break during the hottest hours of the day, but you still must be in fairly good physical shape to participate in this kind of adventure.

336. Go on a photographic safari to Africa.

Just a few decades ago, African safaris typically involved the hunting and killing of big game. Today, however, most safari-goers carry cameras instead of guns. And for good reason. Africa has some of the most stunning scenery and amazing animals on the planet, so a photographic safari to Africa should be at the top of your to-do list. Several international companies offer African photographic tours, and your local travel agent can also provide advice and insight.

Only a handful of Africa's countries are considered mainstream wildlife safari photography destinations. One of the most popular is Kenya, which has more than ten national parks and reserves that are home to a wide diversity of animal species, many of them endangered. Kenya also has a strong tourist infrastructure in place that makes visiting the country relatively easy. Other popular African wildlife photography destinations include Botswana, Namibia, and Tanzania.

> **FUN FACT**
> The word "safari" comes from the Arabic word *safra,* which means "to travel."

If you go on an African adventure, make certain you take a good camera with you and know how to use it. Digital cameras are especially popular because they allow you to take hundreds of photographs on a single card.

❑ 337. See the grandeur of Victoria Falls.

Victoria Falls is one of the Seven Natural Wonders of the World. It is located on the Zambezi River between Zambia and Zimbabwe. Its falls are some of the largest in the world, and it hits its water peak in April during the middle of the rainy season.

When you visit the falls, be sure to swim in the Devil's Armchair. It is both safe and accessible. You will never forget this experience.

❑ *338. Visit the Taj Mahal.*

The spectacular Taj Mahal in Agra, India, was built as a tribute to love and beauty. It's one of the world's best-known and most revered architectural marvels and a must-see vacation destination.

In 1631, Shah Jahan, the fifth Mughal emperor, began the building of the Taj Mahal. It was to be a sacred tomb for his beloved wife, Mumtaz Mahal, who died after bearing him 14 children. It took 22 years to construct and employed more than 20,000 laborers, plus 1,000 elephants to transport the necessary materials. The design and architecture of the Taj Mahal, which means "Crown Palace," is stunning to behold and is renowned for its remarkable workmanship and beauty. Particularly impressive is the building's famous white marble dome surrounded by four tapering minarets. Inside the dome is a jewel-inlaid monument to Mumtaz Mahal.

❏ 339. Visit Mumbai, India, the most populated city in the world.

Never heard of Mumbai? How about Bombay? (Mumbai is what was formerly known to English speakers as Bombay.) In this crowded Indian metropolis, nearly 14 million people inhabit a little more than 1,200 square miles, with between 45,000 and 50,000 persons per square mile. Needless to say, elbow room is at a premium!

Bollywood

Mumbai is the entertainment capital of India. In fact, it is known as "Bollywood," combining the words of Hollywood and Bombay. The film industry in Mumbai produces between 150 and 200 movies per year.

❏ 340. Visit Borobudur, the largest Buddhist temple.

This temple located in Magelang, Central Java, Indonesia, is estimated to have been built in the ninth century A.D. Buddha statues—504 of them—decorate the temple throughout. This great monument is a shrine to the Lord Buddha and an important location for Buddhist pilgrimage. For centuries Borobudur had been buried under volcanic ash and was overgrown with jungle foliage. In the early 1800s, however, a British administration assigned to the region began excavating the temple. Over time, the temple was completely unearthed and in 1973, a major renovation helped to restore it as a place of worship.

341. See Mount Everest, the world's highest mountain.

Situated on the Nepal–Tibet border, Mount Everest in the Himalayas remains the icon of mountain-climbing feats. Its exact height is debated, but it is somewhere between 29,000 and 29,030 feet, the highest point from sea level on the earth's surface.

Kings of the Mountain

- The first known humans to reach the summit of Mount Everest accomplished the feat on May 29, 1953, at 11:30 A.M.

- The team was made up of a Nepalese Sherpa, Tenzing Norgay, and a New Zealander, Sir Edmund Hillary.

- Hillary (a subject of the Queen of England by virtue of her role as head of state in New Zealand) was promptly knighted when the news reached London on the morning of Queen Elizabeth II's coronation day (June 2).

- Tenzing (a subject of Nepal) was awarded the George Medal by the United Kingdom.

342. Make a religious pilgrimage.

For many people, religious faith is the cornerstone of their lives. If spirituality is important to you, make a religious pilgrimage to a holy site in your religion.

There are important holy sites for every world religion. Christians and Jews will both find many throughout Israel. Catholics may also want to visit the Vatican. Devout

Muslims are required to make a pilgrimage to the Saudi Arabian city of Mecca, the most sacred site in Islam, at least once in their lives. This pilgrimage is known as the hajj. Muslims also visit the burial place of the Prophet Muhammad in Medina, Saudi Arabia. Lumbini, situated at the foothills of the Himalayas in modern Nepal, is the alleged birthplace of Siddhartha Gautama, the historical Buddha. For Buddhists, it is the most important holy site to visit. In Hinduism, the Indian city of Varanasi, commonly known as Benares, lies on the holy river Ganges and is said to be the most holy city because so many renowned swamis and gurus have taught there.

■ ■ ■ ■

"Benares is older than history, older than tradition, older even than legend, and looks twice as old as all of them put together."

—Mark Twain

■ ■ ■ ■

❑ *343. Practice tai chi in Tiananmen Square.*

Tai chi is a wonderful way to relieve stress and improve your health. It's extremely popular in China, so consider practicing with the locals in renowned Tiananmen Square. Located near the fabled Forbidden City in downtown Beijing, Tiananmen Square is one of the largest public squares in the world, covering nearly 100 acres. Every day, thousands of people visit the square for their daily exercise, including numerous practitioners of tai chi. You'll also see quite a few walkers, runners, and cyclists.

If possible, plan your trip for spring or early summer. That's when China is at its most beautiful.

❑ 344. See China's terra cotta warriors.

China's ancient history vividly came to life in 1974 with the discovery of thousands of life-size terra cotta warriors and other amazing artifacts in Shaanxi Province. It's one of the most stunning scientific finds in modern history, and it's something not to be missed.

While peasants were digging a well a short distance from the mausoleum of Emperor Qin Shi Huang, who had ascended the throne at the age of 13 in 246 B.C., they discovered the warriors, horses, and chariots. The Museum of Qin Terra Cotta Warriors and Horses was erected at the site, and scientists continue to study the figures for insight into the region's early culture.

The museum is divided into three pits, which were discovered and excavated over a period of several years. In total, more than 7,000 clay soldiers, horses, chariots, and weapons have been unearthed. Most of the soldiers have been restored to their former glory and stand arranged in battle formation, providing a remarkable glimpse of what China's imperial guards looked like eons ago.

❑ 345. Hike the Great Wall of China.

Contrary to legend, you cannot see the Great Wall of China from outer space. You can, however, see this ancient architectural marvel up close by hiking along its many sections. The Great Wall is actually not a single structure, but several connected walls constructed over a period of about 1,800 years, starting in the seventh century B.C., to protect China from invaders. It extends an amazing 4,000 miles westward from the town of Shanhaiguan on the China Sea to Gansu province.

Several companies offer hiking and biking tours along portions of the Great Wall. These excursions can be rustic, with participants often camping on or alongside the Wall. Many shorter hiking opportunities are also available. One of the most popular is a six-mile stretch between Jinshanling and Simatai, 55 miles northeast of Beijing. The trek takes about four hours and is quite challenging because the trail is stony and extremely steep. Well-preserved, easily accessible sections of ancient wall can also be found in Huanghuacheng and Mutianyu.

■ ■ ■ ■

"He who has not climbed the Great Wall is not a true man."

—Mao Zedong

■ ■ ■ ■

❑ 346. Visit the old Imperial Palace in Kyoto.

Japan has a long and fascinating history, with much to keep the casual tourist busy. The next time you're visiting the Land of the Rising Sun, make a special point of traveling to Kyoto and touring the old Imperial Palace.

The palace was the residence of Japan's imperial family until 1868, at which time the capital of Japan—and the emperor—moved to Tokyo. Luckily, the Kyoto Imperial Palace was preserved, and it now offers guided tours hosted by the Imperial Household Agency. Tours in English are conducted twice daily on weekdays and on most Saturdays. No tours are offered on Sundays or on national holidays. If you're a foreign visitor, make sure you bring your passport; it's required to get a ticket.

The Kyoto palace is one of several palaces constructed over the centuries in Kyoto. Fire and other catastrophes had destroyed previous palaces, and the current Kyoto Imperial Palace was the last of its kind to be built there. On the palace grounds are the Imperial Residence, various buildings and halls, and the palace gardens.

The Kyoto Imperial Palace provides a fascinating look into Japan's royal past, and touring it is a fun and educational way to spend a day.

> **FUN FACT**
>
> The current Emperor of Japan is His Imperial Majesty Akihito, the 125th Emperor of Japan, Grand Cordon of the Supreme Order of the Chrysanthemum, Order of the Rising Sun.

❑ 347. Participate in a Japanese tea ceremony.

Japanese culture is rich in tradition and ritual. One of its oldest and most intricate rites is the tea ceremony, which must be experienced to be fully appreciated. If you're ever invited to participate, definitely say yes; you may never get the opportunity again.

FUN FACT

The drinking of hot tea was brought to Japan from China by a Buddhist monk in the ninth century.

Virtually all aspects of the tea ceremony are important, and hosts often spend days going over every tiny detail to make certain that this custom is absolutely correct. The ceremony itself is steeped in ritual, and every step must be performed in a specific order. It can take quite a long time, but the aesthetics of the ceremony are gorgeous to behold.

The Japanese tea ceremony dates back hundreds of years and is still practiced throughout Japan, where the ceremony traditionally takes place in a special room designed specifically for tea. Often the tea room is located in a garden area apart from the main house. In addition to tea, the full ceremony frequently includes a three-course meal with sake. Most Americans have not seen this ceremony, but if you are one of the lucky ones, it has no doubt given you a newfound appreciation for Japanese culture and history. If you're visiting Japan soon, ask your concierge about ceremonial opportunities.

❏ 348. Ride the bullet train by Mount Fuji.

In Japan, the *Shinkansen* is a network of high-speed railway lines. Four Japan Railways Group companies operate this network. Because of their appearance and speed, they are called "bullet trains." They can travel at almost 200 mph.

Mount Fuji is the highest mountain in Japan. The Japanese regard it as a holy mountain. It is also an active volcano that last erupted in the early 18th century. Located in the middle of Japan, it is surrounded by five lakes.

When in Japan, see Mount Fuji while riding in a bullet train. It's an experience you can't pass up.

❏ 349. Hang out with the deer in Nara, Japan.

Deer roam freely in the ancient city of Nara, where they are regarded as divine protectors of the city. Don't be surprised to even see them wander in shops and restaurants. They are actually quite tame. Along with the Kasugayama Primeval Forest, the historic monuments of Nara are declared a UNESCO World Heritage Site.

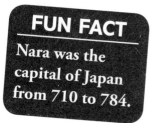

FUN FACT

Nara was the capital of Japan from 710 to 784.

❏ 350. Visit the Hiroshima Peace Memorial Park.

The atomic bombing of Hiroshima, Japan, which helped bring an end to World War II, also ushered in an age of unimaginable destructive power. The centerpiece of the Hiroshima Peace Memorial Park is the Hiroshima Peace Memorial, more commonly known as the Atomic Bomb Dome, over which the bomb exploded on August 6, 1945. Other monuments and buildings of note include:

- The Children's Peace Monument, a statue dedicated to the memory of the children who died in the bombing.

- The Atomic Bomb Memorial Mound, a grass-covered knoll that contains the ashes of 70,000 unidentified victims.

- The Cenotaph for Korean Victims, a monument to the estimated tens of thousands of Koreans living in Hiroshima at the time of the bombing.

- The Memorial Cenotaph, a monument that holds the names of all of the people known to have been killed in the bombing.

- The Peace Flame, which has burned continuously since 1964.

- The Peace Bell, which visitors are encouraged to ring for world peace.

- The Hiroshima National Peace Memorial Hall for the Atomic Bomb Victims, an expression of Japan's desire for lasting peace.

Hiroshima Controversy

The Hiroshima Peace Memorial was designated a UNESCO World Heritage Site in 1996. The United States delegate to the World Heritage Committee abstained from the decision, citing the belief that having a memorial on a war site would influence historical context.

❑ 351. Visit the country of your ancestors.

We're all from somewhere else. True, we may have been born in the United States, but in most cases our heritage hails from far away. Honor your family by visiting the country (or countries) of your ancestors.

If you can, visit the neighborhoods where your distant relatives grew up. Talk to people who knew them. Ask what they were like and about their accomplishments. Don't forget to take photos. By visiting the birthplace of our ancestors, we gain greater knowledge about our family and its place in the world. It also shows us that, at the end of the day, we're all pretty much the same.

■ ■ ■ ■

"My first advice on how not to grow old would be to choose your ancestors carefully."

—Bertrand Russell

■ ■ ■ ■

❑ 352. Visit all seven continents.

The world in which we live is both large and small, depending on how you look at it. Get to know your world better by visiting all seven continents. You do know your continents, don't you? Just to confirm, they're North America, South America, Australia, Europe, Asia, Africa, and Antarctica. The great part about this quest is that no matter where you live, you've already been to one continent!

Each of the continents is amazing in its own way, from its unique and varied cultures to the diversity of its flora and fauna. Each has gorgeous landmarks and a remarkable history just waiting to be explored. And let's not forget the food. With the possible exception of Antarctica, every continent has its own culinary traditions to tempt the taste buds. Of course, you don't have to visit all seven continents at once. Take your time and enjoy them at your leisure. Unlike you, they're not going anywhere.

The Continent of Pangaea

There weren't always seven continents. In the beginning, some scientists believe there was just one giant supercontinent, known as Pangaea. More than 200 million years ago, they say Pangaea broke up into two smaller land masses, and then, through a phenomenon known as continental drift, these two bodies separated into the seven continents we know today.

❑ 353. Climb the highest mountain on each continent.

Life isn't worth living unless it contains challenges that test our mettle and make us better human beings. If your life has been too cushy for too long, commit to the ultimate challenge of climbing the highest mountain on each of the seven continents. Taking on such an extreme endeavor isn't for everyone, of course. It takes physical and mental endurance, not to mention time and money. But if you accomplish this feat, you'll be part of an elite fraternity, and you'll never look at life the same way again.

Rising more than 29,000 feet, the highest mountain in the world is Mount Everest in Nepal, on the continent of

Asia. The highest mountains on the remaining six continents are:

- South America: Mount Aconcagua, Argentina— 22,841 feet
- North America: Mount McKinley (Denali), Alaska— 20,320 feet
- Africa: Mount Kilimanjaro, Tanzania—19,563 feet
- Europe: Mount Elbrus, Russia—18,510 feet
- Antarctica: Vinson Massif—16,066 feet
- Australia: Mount Kosciuski—7,310 feet

Warning: Climbing the world's highest peaks should be attempted only by experienced mountaineers who are in excellent health. But if you're up for it, a variety of mountain-climbing excursions are available worldwide. Consult your travel agent or the Internet for details.

■ ■ ■ ■

"Everest for me, and I believe for the world, is the physical and symbolic manifestation of overcoming odds to achieve a dream."

—Tom Whittaker

■ ■ ■ ■

❏ 354. Live in a foreign country.

If you're single and relatively unencumbered, consider living in a foreign country for a year. It's a great way to see what the rest of the world has to offer. Moving abroad, however, is not something you should do on the spur of the moment.

It requires planning and resources. You'll need a passport and a visa, as well as a plan on how to support yourself.

If money isn't an issue, consider your year abroad as an opportunity to relax, have fun, and immerse yourself in a foreign culture, but if you're like most people, you'll have to get a job. If you have a special skill, such as nursing, find out if it's needed in the country you'd like to visit. If you don't have a special skill, inquire about a job teaching English—it's a gig in high demand right now.

Make the best use of your time abroad. Put away the phrase book and make an honest attempt at learning the native language. Go out of your way to meet people and make friends. See the sights and learn the nation's history. Moving abroad for a long period is a big decision, but one that will have a huge impact on your life and future. So go for it.

❑ 355. Stay in a hostel in another country.

The hostel culture is a little different than the luxury hotel circuit. Well . . . okay, it's a lot different. Travelers on a budget from all over the world avail themselves of these often quaint and unique accommodations. Work a stay into your itinerary sometime. It's a kick!

❑ 356. Visit the North Pole.

Ever dream of visiting Santa Claus at the North Pole? Well, Santa may be just a fantasy, but a trip to the top of the world doesn't have to be. Start saving now for the vacation of a lifetime!

Today, the North Pole is a major tourist destination, and numerous companies offer excursions that would have amazed early explorers. Both overland and sea expeditions are available, depending on how adventuresome you feel, and one company even offers the opportunity to skydive over the North Pole from a special helicopter.

Consult the Internet or your travel agent for North Pole travel opportunities.

❑ 357. Visit the South Pole.

Once you've got a trip to the North Pole under your belt, journey to the opposite extreme and visit the South Pole! Keep in mind that a trip to the South Pole isn't for the faint of heart. The region is extremely cold and somewhat difficult to access. But once you're there, you'll witness sights that others have seen only on television, including a spectacular array of Antarctic wildlife, glaciers, and stunning ice formations.

Unlike the North Pole, which is essentially a giant sheet of ice, the South Pole is solid ground. It's been the location of a manned research station since 1956, and in recent years has become a very popular tourist destination. Several companies offer excursions that take you there by sea, including two-week cruises that leave out of South America. The South Pole is one of the last,

vast undeveloped regions on Earth. Don't pass up an opportunity to see it up close.

❏ 358. Cross the International Date Line.

Want to travel in time? Cross the International Date Line! It's an imaginary line in the middle of the Pacific Ocean that runs from the North Pole to the South Pole and is 180 degrees away from the Greenwich Meridian. The line separates two consecutive days, so if you're immediately to the left of the International Date Line (in the Eastern Hemisphere), you're one day ahead of the day

Crooked Time

The International Date Line is not a perfectly straight line. In fact, it has been adjusted several times over the years to accommodate certain islands and countries in the Pacific Ocean. For example, it bends slightly to include all of Kirbari in the Eastern Hemisphere.

that's immediately to the right of the line (in the Western Hemisphere).

Cruise ships often cross the International Date Line as part of their passage, and some celebrate with parties and other festivities. So have a good time, and make sure you brag about your achievement when you return home.

❑ *359. Take a cruise.*

Some quick questions: Do you enjoy being pampered? Sightseeing in exotic locations? Relaxing in a cool ocean breeze? These experiences and more can be yours when you take a cruise. Don't worry,

FUN FACT

More than 10,000,000 people take a cruise each year. About 80 percent do it in North American waters.

you're not limited to just cruising the Caribbean, though numerous Caribbean cruises are available if that's your wish. Today's cruises take you all over the world, from Alaska to the Mediterranean and all ports in between. Best of all, cruises have never been cheaper. So why wait? Consult your travel agent to see which cruise is right for you.

❑ *360. Collect sea shells on a foreign beach.*

A glimpse of the fascinating undersea world appears on shores around the world each time the tide recedes. Beachcombers—people who search the shoreline for what the tide has left behind—are often shell seekers who enjoy identifying or collecting the sea's own unique treasures. The quest for new or perfect specimens can quickly become an enjoyable and relaxing obsession as the sound of the waves accompanies the hunt. You may not be able to take your collection home with you (some beaches do not permit it, and airport customs may forbid it), but the pleasure of the experience will remain with you.

Beachcombing Tips

Useful tools: A pail or other small container, a small digging tool, and a magnifying glass.

Helpful techniques: Take your time and look carefully; dig gently into sand and mud; replace any rocks you overturn; don't remove living organisms; handle organisms with care; use moderation in the number of nonliving shells and organisms you take home.

❑ 361. Scuba dive in the Great Barrier Reef.

Australia's Great Barrier Reef is one of nature's most impressive wonders, and there's no better way to enjoy it than below the surface, face to face with the critters that live there.

Spanning more than 133,000 square miles in the Pacific Ocean, the Great Barrier Reef is home to a remarkable diversity of creatures, including more than 1,500 different species of fish, 400 different corals, 5,000 species of mollusks, and 10,000 species of sponges. You'll also find several types of sharks, dolphins, turtles, and even seasonal sightings of migrating whales. Best of all, the water is so clear that you can see practically forever.

The Great Barrier Reef actually comprises more than 3,000 individual reef systems and coral cays, and literally hundreds of tropical islands, almost all of which have sun-soaked, golden beaches. It's no wonder that the Great Barrier Reef is one of Australia's most popular attractions.

Scuba diving and snorkeling allow you to get up close and personal with the vast array of sea life that calls the Great Barrier Reef home, and several Australia-based companies offer day-length and longer excursions. Contact your local travel agent for details and itineraries.

❑ 362. Climb the Sydney Harbor Bridge.

The Sydney Harbor Bridge is one of Australia's most famous urban attractions. And climbing it is an adventure everyone should undertake (unless you have a fear of heights). Two different 3.5-hour climbing opportunities are available:

The Sydney Harbor Bridge

The Sydney Harbor Bridge was opened on March 19, 1932. It's the world's largest steel arch bridge and is 3,769 feet long, including approach spans. The bridge took six years to construct, contains six million hand-driven rivets, and has a painted surface area equal to 60 football fields.

- The Bridge Climb takes you along catwalks and up ladders as you steadily ascend toward the summit, 440 feet above Sydney Harbor. From the peak you'll have a spectacular 360-degree view of Sydney and the surrounding area, including the world-renowned Sydney Opera House.

- The Discovery Climb offers a unique look at the engineering and design of the Sydney Harbor Bridge. You're taken to the summit of the suspension arch of the bridge, winding around supporting structures and climbing the staircases that join the two arches.

❑ 363. Go on a walkabout in Australia.

Australia is a remarkable country, and it's so large that it's actually considered a continent. It features some of the most astounding flora and fauna in the world, and the best way to enjoy it is through a walkabout.

Of course, we're not talking about a traditional Aboriginal walkabout, which is an ancient spiritual rite of passage in which a young person lives in the wilderness for an extended period of time. Instead, we're referring to a visit to Australia that takes you out of the big city and into the wild, where you can see animals in their natural environment and marvel at Australia's remarkable landscape. The longer you spend there, the better. But to fully enjoy all that Australia has to offer, you should plan to be there no less than a week.

Several companies offer extended excursions into Australia's famous back country, and most place their focus on close encounters with the continent's many unique animals, including kangaroos, wombats, and koalas. Consult your travel agent for tour information.

❑ 364. Visit New Zealand, where The Lord of the Rings trilogy was filmed.

To many filmgoers, New Zealand is Middle Earth, because New Zealand–born Peter Jackson filmed the entire three movies of *The Lord of the Rings* in diverse locations throughout this country. In fact, he used the hills of Matamata as

Hobbiton, the volcanic region of Mount Ruapehu as the fiery Mount Doom where Sauron forged The One Ring, and Queenstown as the setting of the Eregion Hills and the Pillars of Argonath. But even if you haven't seen any of these movies, it's worth your time to see the unspoiled and wondrous beauty of New Zealand.

❑ *365. Visit Easter Island.*

There are a lot of bizarre phenomena around the world, and some of the most unusual are the huge stone statues on Easter Island in the South Pacific. If you've seen them only in photographs, you owe yourself a visit. A total of 887 stone statues, known as *moai,* have been uncovered on Easter Island. Though often referred to as "Easter Island heads," the statues are actually complete torsos. Many have been buried up to their heads by shifting sand.

❑ *366. Snorkel in the Caribbean.*

If you can't visit the Great Barrier Reef in Australia, consider a snorkeling vacation in the Caribbean. Here are a few suggestions:

■ Bonaire Marine Park, Bonaire: Wade from the shore off your hotel onto stunning coral reefs.

■ Stingray City, Grand Cayman: Frolic with dozens of gentle stingrays in crystal-clear water.

- St. Martin: Visit the French side of the island, where the government strives to keep the waters pure and undisturbed.

- Provo, Turks, and Caicos: Snorkeling trails at Smith's Reef and Bight Reef off Grace Bay Beach provide access to gorgeous coral gardens.

❑ 367. Visit Lake Texcoco in central Mexico.

The Aztec Empire comprised several city-states, and the most prominent is Tenochtitlán, which is on Lake Texcoco and was founded in 1325. The empire itself reigned supreme in this area until the Spanish conquest in 1521. Its most famous leader was Hueyi Tlatoani Moctezuma II. Today, people can visit the Aztec ruins and learn about its culture and history.

❑ 368. Cruise the Panama Canal.

Cruises can take you all over the world. For your next vacation, consider passage through the historic Panama Canal! The 48-mile waterway connects the Atlantic and Pacific oceans, and it remains one of the most impressive and costly modern engineering feats ever attempted. The project took a total of 34 years from the first attempt by France in 1880 to the canal's official opening in 1914, and it required the labor of 80,000 men.

Think about that as you're enjoying a cool drink on your balcony.

❏ 369. Visit some Mayan ruins.

From about A.D. 300 to 900, Mayan civilization flourished in parts of what is now southern Mexico, Guatemala, Belize, El Salvador, and western Honduras. The Mayans built some stunning temples, created a system of writing, and practiced astronomy with a precision that put Europeans to shame.

FUN FACT

The Mayans developed a highly efficient system of mathematics based on the number 20 (rather than the base-10 system we use). They wrote complex numbers using just three symbols: a shell (zero), a dot (one), and a line (five).

❏ 370. Cruise the Amazon River.

The Amazon is one of the mightiest rivers in the world, an incredibly vast waterway that empties billions of gallons of fresh water into the ocean each year. It flows through several South American countries and provides cruise opportunities like no other river.

Excursions are plentiful and can take you upstream or downstream. A variety of departures are available in Bolivia, Brazil, Equador, and Peru, so your biggest decision will be where to start. Your travel agent can give you the particulars and help you chart an itinerary that gives you the biggest bang for your buck.

The Amazon has long been steeped in mystery, which is half the fun. It courses through dense rainforest and past big cities and tiny native villages. Along the way, you'll see a remarkable array of wildlife, including chattering monkeys, colorful birds, huge reptiles, and fish that appear to have jumped straight out of a science-fiction movie. No matter how much you've read about the Amazon River, nothing can prepare you for the awesome experience you'll enjoy on a week-long river cruise.

❑ 371. Visit the Galapagos Islands.

You want to see historical islands that had a crucial impact on science? Then visit the famous Galapagos Islands, where a remarkable diversity of plants and animals inspired Charles Darwin's theory of evolution by natural selection. The islands are a living, breathing natural laboratory, and something you absolutely must see to believe.

Located off the coast of Ecuador, the Galapagos chain comprises 13 major islands, of which five are currently inhabited. A spectacular array of animals call the islands home, including the giant, gentle Galapagos tortoises; land and marine iguanas; flightless cormorants; blue-footed boobys; Galapagos penguins; waved albatrosses; and Galapagos sea lions.

The Galapagos archipelago is a popular tourist destination, and a variety of excursions are available to visitors. (Your travel agent can help you make the necessary arrangements.) The islands have been greatly abused over the past century, but a strong conservancy movement is now in place to protect the native species and bring the islands back to their former glory. So remember: Take all the photos you want, but make sure that's all you take!

372. Visit Machu Picchu.

Lost cities attract adventurers like a magnet, but you don't have to be Indiana Jones to visit the fabled Machu Picchu in Peru. Located more than 8,000 feet above sea level on a mountain ridge above the Urubamba Valley, Machu Picchu is a popular destination spot for those who make it their life mission to visit the most amazing places on Earth.

Constructed around 1460, the so-called Lost City of the Incas was abandoned by Incan rulers about a century later. It was rediscovered in 1911 by Hiram Bingham, a historian at Yale University, though there is strong evidence that decades earlier others had visited (and possibly plundered) Machu Picchu.

Archaeologists believe Machu Picchu was a royal estate and religious retreat. It contains approximately 200 buildings including temples and is believed to have been home to approximately 1,200 people. One of the highlights of the site is the *intihuatana,* a column of rock used by Incan priests to "tie the sun" during the winter solstice. Spanish invaders destroyed most of the intihuatana, but the one at Machu Picchu was spared because of its remote location.

373. See Christ the Redeemer statue in Rio de Janeiro.

The statue known as Christ the Redeemer, which overlooks Rio de Janiero, is one of Brazil's most famous landmarks. Someday soon, make a pilgrimage and see it for yourself.

Standing 120 feet tall, the reinforced concrete-and-soapstone monument looms over Rio from its location at the peak of Corcovado Mountain in the Tijuca Forest

National Park. The statue took nine years to construct at a cost of $250,000 and was dedicated on October 12, 1931.

Christ the Redeemer is the second-largest statue of its kind in the world. Only the statue of Cristo de la Concordia in Cochabamba, Bolivia, is taller—by inches.

❑ 374. Attend Carnival in Rio de Janeiro.

Carnival in Rio de Janeiro, Brazil, is the most famous and colorful international celebration you'll ever attend. So find an appropriate costume and make plans for next year's party!

Traditionally held 40 days before Easter, Rio Carnival is a wild four-day celebration highlighted by outrageous parades, masquerade parties, and balls. It officially starts on Saturday and concludes on Fat Tuesday with the beginning of Lent.

Carnival is a very big deal in Brazil, and Rio is home to some of the nation's biggest, most elaborate parades and events. In fact, more than 100 parades fill the city's streets over the four-day holiday, many of which encourage viewers to participate. Parade participants dress up in flamboyant costumes and tens of thousands of people gather to celebrate. Large festivities are also held in the cities of Salvador, Porto Seguro, and Recife.

Because Carnival attracts large crowds from around the world, it's wise to make your travel plans early to guarantee that you get the accommodations you want. Don't assume that you can simply show up at the beginning of the celebration, because all area hotel rooms will likely be filled. Your travel agent can help you make the necessary arrangements.

❏ *375. Watch soccer in Brazil.*

Soccer is an international sport, but few countries take the game as seriously as Brazil. If work or vacation takes you to Brazil, ask your hotel concierge about getting tickets to a local match. It'll be one of the most exciting events you've ever attended. And if you're a fan, you haven't lived until you've cheered with a Brazilian crowd.

Soccer matches are easy to find throughout Brazil— those featuring the national team are the best attended. Be wary of over-the-top fans, however. Sometimes their passion for the game, especially during international matches, can explode into unsportsmanlike behavior.

■ ■ ■ ■

"Whoever invented [soccer] should be worshiped as a god."

—Hugo Sanchez, Mexican soccer player and coach

■ ■ ■ ■

❑ 376. Play soccer.

Baseball may be the Great American Pastime, but soccer is the most popular sport in the world. Known internationally as football, soccer is a game with a long and storied history. But unlike the

American sport of football, soccer players, with the exception of the goalie, cannot touch the ball with their hands, which makes for more complicated play.

Soccer has become increasingly popular in the United States, and most municipalities host amateur leagues. Check with your local parks and recreation department to see what's available in your area.

❑ 377. Attend a boxing match.

Boxing is a sport that you either love or hate. If you've never witnessed a professional match in person, however, it's time you saw what all the fuss is about. Yell your lungs out—and be glad it's not you in the ring.

> **"Boxing is the toughest and loneliest sport in the world."**
>
> —Frank Bruno

❑ 378. Learn to fence.

You don't have to be a Musketeer to take up fencing. It's a fun sport that almost anyone can enjoy, and fencing schools and clubs are available throughout the United States.

Fencing can involve a variety of weapons. The foil is most commonly associated with the sport, but the epee and saber are also popular. When joining a fencing class or club, make sure it offers a good mix of beginner, intermediate, and advanced fencers. That way, as you become more proficient, you'll always have someone of equal (or greater) skill with whom to practice.

❑ 379. Go target shooting.

Archery and firearm ranges afford safe places to try out or hone your shooting skills. The idea of hunting doesn't appeal to everyone, but target shooting is a skill you can impress your friends with at the fair, and maybe win a stuffed animal.

❑ 380. Attend the Olympics.

When it comes to athletics, there are few events more exciting than the Summer and Winter Olympic Games. They're a must-see for anyone who truly enjoys watching top athletes compete.

According to historians, the first Olympic Games occurred around 776 B.C. They were dedicated to the Olympian gods and took place on the ancient plains of Olympia. The games continued for nearly 1,200 years until Emperor Theodosius decreed in A.D. 393 that all such "pagan cults" be banned.

The first modern Olympic Games were held in Athens in 1896 and have continued every four years with the exception of 1940 and 1944, when the Games were canceled because of World War II. The first Winter Olympic Games were held in Chamonix, France, in 1924. The Summer and Winter Olympics now alternate every two years.

The XXI Olympic Winter Games will be held in Vancouver, Canada, in 2010, and the XXII Olympic Winter Games will be hosted by Sochi, Russia, in 2014. The XXX Olympic Summer Games will be held in London, England, in 2012. Consult your travel agent for ticket and travel information. And to learn more about the Olympic Games, visit www.olympic.org.

❑ 381. Attend a major tennis tournament.

Tennis fans tend to be obsessive about their favorite sport. Show your passion for the game by attending one of the four Grand Slam tournaments: the Australian Open, French Open, Wimbledon, and the U.S. Open.

The fun starts with the Australian Open, which is held each January in Melbourne Park. The tournament started in

1905, and from that year through 1987, tennis was played on grass. Today, the Australian Open is played on a hard court.

The French Open follows in mid-May with two weeks of play at the Stade Roland Garros in Paris. Games are played on clay courts, and the tourney's five-set men's singles matches on these courts are considered some of the most physically demanding in professional tennis.

Next is Wimbledon, which is traditionally played in late June and early July at the All England Club in Wimbledon, a suburb of London. Wimbledon is arguably the most prestigious tennis tournament in the world and one of the most watched on television.

Last is the U.S. Open, a hard-court tournament played in August and September at the USTA Billie Jean King National Tennis Center in Queens, New York. The U.S. Open has a rich history and has been held since 1881.

■ ■ ■ ■

"I have always considered tennis as a combat in an arena between two gladiators who have their racquets and their courage as their weapons."

—Yannick Noah

■ ■ ■ ■

❏ 382. Play racquetball.

Did you abandon tennis because you got tired of chasing after missed or stray balls? Then racquetball is for you! Actually, racquetball is for anyone who enjoys swinging a racquet. It's a fast-paced indoor game, and the beauty of it is that all of the surfaces of the fully enclosed court (floor, ceiling, and walls) are legal playing surfaces. Generally play is between two players, but you can even have

fun practicing your skills by yourself. Don't forget to wear eye protection, though! The little blue rubber ball may look harmless enough, but high velocity tends to change that.

❏ 383. Attend a major golf tournament.

Are you a big Tiger Woods fan? Or do you think Jack Nicklaus is still the greatest golfer? Or perhaps golf holds no interest for you at all? In any case, you'll be thrilled at any of golf's majors: the Masters (April), U.S. Open (June), British Open (July), and PGA Championship (August). The beauty of a golf course at a major tournament is breathtaking!

❏ 384. Play a round of golf at Augusta.

It's the dream of every avid golfer to play a round at the ultra-exclusive Augusta National Golf Club in Augusta, Georgia. Perhaps someday this dream will come true for you.

Founded by Bobby Jones and Clifford Roberts with courses designed by Alister MacKenzie, the Augusta National Golf Club opened for play in 1933. It currently has approximately 300 members, including many of business and industry's biggest names. The club offers one championship 18-hole course and one nine-hole course.

Augusta National Golf Club is a private club. As a result, there are basically three ways to find yourself playing there: be selected to play in the annual Masters Golf Tournament (probably your least likely opportunity, unless you're a top professional), be a member of the club (which is by invitation only), or be invited to play by a member. But don't fret if the Augusta National Golf Club won't let you play. The region is home to several gorgeous public courses that will welcome you with open arms.

Discrimination at Augusta

After facing public criticism over allegedly discriminatory admissions, Augusta National Golf Club accepted its first black member in 1990. In 2002, the club was challenged over its policy of excluding women, though women are allowed to play as guests of members.

❏ 385. Attend the Kentucky Derby.

The Kentucky Derby has been called the most exciting two minutes in sports, and with good reason. It's one of the most famous horse races in the world, and you don't have to bet the farm to have a great time.

The Kentucky Derby is held at Churchill Downs in Louisville, Kentucky, on the first Saturday in May, and concludes the two-week Kentucky Derby Festival. It's the first leg of the Triple Crown of Thoroughbred Racing and is followed by the Preakness Stakes and the Belmont Stakes.

Horse racing in Kentucky has a rich history dating back to 1789, when the first racecourse was established in Lexington. Churchill Downs opened in 1875, and the first Kentucky Derby was held in May of that year.

Horse racing is just one aspect of the Kentucky Derby. Over the years, it has turned into a huge affair with parties, balls, and other activities that draw thousands to Louisville. As for the race itself, tickets are relatively easy to acquire and can be purchased well in advance. You should also book your hotel room as early as you can, due to the large number of people who descend on Louisville at Derby time.

■ ■ ■ ■

"If Jack Nicklaus can win the Masters at 46, I can win the Kentucky Derby at 54."

—jockey Willie Shoemaker

■ ■ ■ ■

❑ *386. Attend a World Series.*

There's no greater thrill among baseball fans than the World Series. It's the culmination of a hard-fought 162-game season (plus playoffs), and every baseball fan worth his horsehide should attend at least one World Series game.

The first official World Series occurred in 1903, but the sport had some version of a post-season championship long before. In 1884, the Providence Grays of the National League defeated the New York Metropolitan Club of the American Association in a three-game series known as the

Championship of the United States. Several sportswriters referred to the Grays as "world champions," and the title stuck. Over the next six years, some type of a championship series, ranging from 6 to 15 games, took place between the National League and American Association pennant winners.

Today, the World Series is a best-of-seven championship between the pennant winners of the American League and the National League. Tickets sell quickly, but World Series packages can often be purchased through a ticket broker.

❏ 387. Watch the Bronx Bombers play at the new Yankee Stadium.

The old Yankee Stadium was one of the most hallowed sites in Major League Baseball. So even if you're not a Yankees fan, you owe it to yourself to enjoy a ball game at the new Yankee Stadium, which is intended to reflect the grandeur of the old stadium. Commonly known as "The House That Ruth Built" after home run king Babe Ruth, the old Yankee Stadium has been home to dozens of Hall of Famers, and the location of some of the most exciting moments in baseball history.

The Yankees moved to a brand new park with the 2009 season, after 85 glorious years at the old Yankee Stadium. The decision shocked many longtime Yankees fans, who just couldn't imagine watching baseball anywhere else. The new park, however, is located just across the street from the old one and features the same field dimensions, so little has changed.

❑ 388. Watch the Red Sox play at Fenway Park.

Fenway is one of baseball's most treasured baseball parks. The next time you're there, do your best to snag a foul ball. It's a thrill of a lifetime!

Of course, catching a foul ball is a matter of luck—that is, being in the right place at the right time. As with all ball parks, the best way to increase your odds at Fenway Park is by sitting along the first or third baseline. (A screen protects fans sitting behind home plate.) And don't forget your glove—it'll help keep you from dropping whatever balls fly your way.

The Opening of Fenway

The first professional baseball game ever played in Fenway Park took place on April 20, 1912. The Boston Red Sox defeated the New York Highlanders (later known as the Yankees) 7–6 in 11 innings. A highlight of the game was a Tris Speaker home run.

❑ 389. See the lovable Cubbies play at Wrigley Field.

Wrigley Field, home of the Chicago Cubs, is the second-oldest Major League baseball park after Fenway Park in Boston. For a truly fun afternoon, watch a game there—from the bleachers.

FUN FACT

Wrigley Field was originally known as Weeghman Park.

Wrigley Field is rich in baseball history. It's where Babe Ruth allegedly called his home run shot in Game 3 of the 1932 World Series and where the Cubs' Hippo Vaughn and Fred Toney of the Cincinnati Reds both pitched no-hitters through the 9th inning on May 2, 1917.

❑ 390. Visit the Baseball Hall of Fame.

Every sport has its mecca—that holy place where fans come to worship the greats. Among baseball buffs, it's the National Baseball Hall of Fame and Museum in Cooperstown, New York. Dedicated on June 12, 1939, the National Baseball Hall of Fame and Museum honors the sport's greatest talents and chronicles its history from a simple game of stick-and-ball to the Great American Pastime.

FUN FACT

In 1936, the first class of baseball greats was elected into the Baseball Hall of Fame. Ty Cobb, Babe Ruth, Honus Wagner, Christy Mathewson, and Walter Johnson made up this class, but they weren't inducted until the opening commencement in 1939.

The Hall of Fame can't be done in a single day; there's just too much to see. In the Plaque Gallery, visitors can gaze at images of baseball's greatest players, managers, and executives and read about the accomplishments that brought them there. In the 50,000-square-foot Museum, you'll find a remarkable array of artifacts, including bats, balls, uniforms, and other memorabilia dating back to baseball's earliest days. The Museum also features a variety of special exhibits that touch on everything from the evolution of the game and the fan experience to Major League parks and baseball's influence on Hollywood.

❑ 391. Attend a baseball fantasy camp.

If you love baseball—and who doesn't?—dust off your mitt and play with the pros at a baseball fantasy camp!

Many major league teams host camps during the off-season in which fans can suit up, learn the basics, and play real games beside their baseball heroes. It's the vacation of a lifetime because you don't have to be skilled at the sport; all you need to have fun is spirit, hustle, and a love of the game.

Most fantasy baseball camps last about a week. During that time, you get to play the game just as the major leaguers do, usually on the team's home field using regulation equipment. You'll make a lot of new friends and come home with some amazing souvenirs—and even more amazing memories.

Some teams also offer international trips that allow you to play in baseball-loving countries such as Costa Rica and China. These camps obviously cost more than those in the States, but the opportunities for fun are also greater.

❑ 392. Attend a college bowl game.

Have you ever sat in a college football stadium with more than a hundred thousand fans screaming their heads off? It's especially deafening during a college football bowl game, and it's an experience not to be passed up.

Each year it seems as though a new bowl is played, so that now there are about 40 college bowls played throughout the country. That means about 80 college football squads play in the post-season. Of course, every college football player aspires to play in one of the major bowls, particularly the BCS (Bowl Championship Series) National Championship Game. The other four major bowls are the Orange Bowl (outside Miami, Florida), the Sugar Bowl (New Orleans, Louisiana), the Fiesta Bowl (Glendale, Arizona), and the granddaddy of all bowls, the Rose Bowl (Pasadena, California).

The pageantry of these games is reason enough to experience them, but if you can't attend one, then go to a bowl near you, especially if your school's football team is a participant. And remember, it's perfectly acceptable to scream your head off at a college bowl game.

❏ *393. Visit the Pro Football Hall of Fame.*

Canton, Ohio, isn't the biggest city in the Buckeye State, but as the home of the Pro Football Hall of Fame, it sees more than its share of tourists. Every devoted football fan should make at least one pilgrimage to this popular sports museum.

The Pro Football Hall of Fame honors the sport of football and its brightest stars. In 1963, it opened its doors with a charter class of 17 inductees, and over the years it has undergone three major renovations, expanding from 19,000 to 83,000 square feet. The Hall boasts an eclectic array of displays, including the Moments, Memories & Mementos Gallery and the Pro Football Today Gallery, which houses four main exhibits: NFL Goes Global, The Pro Bowl, Rookie Records, and Career Records. You can also watch thrilling game highlights in the Hall's theater.

Host City

People often wonder how Canton, Ohio, came to host the Pro Football Hall of Fame. There are actually several reasons. One, the American Professional Football Association, later known as the National Football League, was founded in Canton in September 1920. In addition, the Canton Bulldogs were among the best teams during the early years of professional football, winning championships in 1922 and 1923.

❑ *394. Attend the Super Bowl.*

It's the sporting event of the year, and almost everyone watches it—even people who don't like football. It's the Super Bowl, and you should attend at least one before you head for that big end zone in the sky.

The Super Bowl is the championship game of the National Football League (NFL), though it didn't start out that way. The first Super Bowl was played on January 15, 1967, between the champion teams of the NFL and the rival American Football League (AFL). When the leagues merged in 1970, the Super Bowl became a championship game between the NFL's two conferences, the American Football Conference and the National Football Conference.

The Super Bowl is generally the most-watched and highest-rated television broadcast of the year, but it is best enjoyed in person. Unless you're friends with someone in high places, however, expect to pay a pretty penny for your ticket. On the plus side, you'll be able to brag to all of your friends, "I was there."

If there's a downside to watching the Super Bowl in person, it's this: You'll miss all those hilarious commercials.

❏ 395. Visit the Basketball Hall of Fame.

Over the past century, basketball has grown to become one of the nation's most popular sports, both on the professional and college levels. The greats of the sport are enshrined at the Naismith Memorial Basketball Hall of Fame in Springfield, Massachusetts. If you're a fan of basketball and have never visited, you owe it to yourself to do so.

The Hall pays tribute to the history of basketball, its evolution and growth,

Basketball's Beginning

In 1891, Canadian physical education instructor James Naismith invented the game of basketball. The sport first used soccer balls, which were dribbled and tossed into a peach basket. The steel hoop and mesh net now associated with basketball were introduced two years later.

and its most talented and influential players and coaches. Although the Hall was established in 1959, its actual physical site didn't open to the public until 1968 at Springfield College. Later, the Hall moved to its current location on the banks of the Connecticut River in 1985. As with all the other major sports halls of fame, the Naismith Memorial Basketball Hall of Fame offers a remarkable look at all aspects of the sport. Exhibits include the Honors Ring, with photos and memorabilia from all inductees; a Players Gallery; a Coaches Gallery; and a College Section.

❑ 396. See the Harlem Globetrotters play basketball.

Basketball has never been more fun than watching the Harlem Globetrotters do their thing on the basketball court. If you have never seen them make passes, shoot baskets, and clown around, then you are in for a treat of a lifetime. You will never laugh so much.

In the 1920s, Abe Saperstein formed this hugely popular exhibition team in Chicago, Illinois. He named the club after Harlem in New York because of its connections with the African American community. The Globetrotters have since played more than 20,000 exhibition games in 118 countries.

FUN FACT

Both Wilt "the Stilt" Chamberlain and Earvin "Magic" Johnson played for the Globetrotters.

❑ 397. Visit the Hockey Hall of Fame.

Hockey is to Canada what baseball is to the United States—a national obsession. Hockey fans get their puck on at the Hockey Hall of Fame in Toronto, Canada, but before its existence, calls for a hockey hall of fame date back to 1940. After several false starts, an official Hockey Hall of Fame opened at the Canadian National Exhibition in Toronto in 1961. It moved to its current location at Brookfield Place in Toronto in 1993.

The Hall offers much for the diehard hockey fan. Of special note is the NHL Zone, which is guarded by larger-than-life statues of hockey legends Cyclone Taylor and Ken Dryden. Here you'll find photos and artifacts from the Hall of Fame's most honored members, including Wayne Gretzky, Gordie Howe, Bobby Orr, and Mario Lemieux, as well as the most recent inductees. Other popular exhibits include NHL Today, which showcases current NHL players; NHL Retro, which takes a detailed look at franchise histories; and NHL Milestones, which highlights hockey's most impressive records, including Darryl Sittler's ten-point game and Terry Sawchuk's 103 shutouts.

■ ■ ■ ■

"Ice hockey is a form of disorderly conduct in which the score is kept."

—Doug Larson

■ ■ ■ ■

❑ *398. Attend a Stanley Cup championship game.*

The Stanley Cup is named after Frederick Stanley, who was an avid fan of ice hockey and who donated a decorative bowl to the sport. In 1893, the trophy was first awarded to the Montreal Hockey Club for their championship season, but the club refused it. Later, the Ottawa Senators became the first National Hockey League (NHL) championship team to receive the Cup in 1927. Since then, the Montreal Canadians have won the Cup an amazing 24 times. No other team has come close.

The NHL championship series is truly a thrilling sporting experience. You can't help but get caught up in the excitement of players racing down the rink while the puck skims across the ice.

❑ *399. Enter the Iditarod.*

The Iditarod is much more than just a dog sled race—it's a grueling test of endurance that challenges the stoutest of hearts and spirits. If you think you have what it takes, sign up and prove it.

Often called the "last great race on Earth," the Iditarod covers 1,150 miles from Anchorage to Nome. Along the way, mushers and their dogs cross some of the most brutal—and beautiful—terrain in Alaska, including jagged mountains, frozen

The Iditarod Trail

The Iditarod Trail was originally a mail and supply route from the coastal towns of Seward and Knik through the mining camps of Flat, Ophir, and Ruby, and on to the western communities. In 1925, the trail was used to deliver serum via sled dog to diphtheria-ravaged Nome, saving many lives.

rivers, and barren tundra. The race typically takes from 10 to 17 days, and it is definitely not for the faint of heart.

Mushers come from around the world and from all walks of life. Men and women compete side by side, and may the best person—and dog team—win. Participation, however, does not come cheap. Mushers must pay an entry fee of $4,000, which includes Iditarod and P.R.I.D.E. (Providing Responsible Information on a Dog's Environment) membership.

❑ *400. Go surfing in Hawaii.*

It's almost a cliché, but if surfing is your thing, you definitely should hit the waves off Hawaii. After all, it's where the sport was born. The waves are their most tantalizing in Hawaii from November to March. Each of the Hawaiian islands receives its share of good-size swells, which can range from 10 to 30 feet, so your biggest decision will be where to go. The famous North Shore on the island of Oahu is best-known among international surfers and is one of the best places to watch surfers in action.

If you've never surfed before, Hawaii is also a great place to take lessons.

■ ■ ■

"Surfing is very much like making love. It always feels good, no matter how many times you've done it."
—Paul Strauch

■ ■ ■

❑ *401. Go fishing.*

Some people like to fish from a boat. Other people like to cast their line while standing on a shore or pier or while wading in a stream. Some people like to catch tuna or marlin from the ocean. Other people like to reel in trout or catfish from a lake. You may like to do all of these things, or you may not have enjoyed any of these pleasures. Whatever you have or haven't done, go fishing today! It's an activity that is sure to lure you in.

❑ *402. Go noodling.*

If fishing with a rod and reel has lost its appeal, go noodling!

Popular in the South, noodling is a technique for catching catfish that involves using one's fingers as bait. Find a possible catfish hole (submerged logs are very popular), stick your hand in, wiggle your fingers, and wait for a catfish to grab it. Sure, it can be a little painful, but noodling can help you land some very large fish.

Noodling is illegal in some states, so check with your local Fish and Game Department before you try it. And noodle only in shallow water—large catfish can be strong enough to pull you under.

■ ■ ■ ■

"It has always been my private conviction that any man who pits his intelligence against a fish and loses has it coming."

—John Steinbeck

■ ■ ■ ■

403. Go ice fishing.

If you live by a large lake where it snows, embrace winter by grabbing your long johns, a drill, and a fishing pole. Then go ice fishing! The fish don't mind the brisk temperatures, so you shouldn't either.

404. Go deep-sea fishing.

Any day on the ocean is a day well spent. Throw in some deep-sea fishing, and you've got a little slice of heaven. You don't have to be a seasoned angler to enjoy deep-sea fishing. Most professional deep-sea charters take care of the grunt work for you—positioning the boat for optimum casting, baiting your hook, and even helping you reel in your catch if it's especially big.

FUN FACT

The largest hook-caught blue marlin on record was snagged in the Atlantic Ocean. It weighed a whopping 1,402 pounds!

Deep-sea fishing is popular in the United States and throughout the world. Moreover, day, weekend, and week-long excursions are readily available along both American coasts and the Gulf of Mexico. Charters can also be found throughout the Caribbean, especially at popular tourist resorts. The fish that can be caught while deep-sea fishing range from sailfish and marlin to tuna and grouper.

The benefits of deep-sea fishing are many. They include the opportunity to enjoy a day in the sun, to bond with family and friends, and to experience the singular thrill of landing a truly impressive trophy fish. In addition, if your catch is edible, such as tuna or grouper, you'll come home with a cooler full of choice fillets.

So join the many anglers who sail the seven seas and make new friends in your quest for the big one!

❑ 405. Go whitewater rafting.

Whitewater rafting can be a thrill-a-minute adventure. Isn't it time you took the plunge? Sure, river rafting carries certain inherent risks, but for most enthusiasts that's part of the fun. (If you wanted to stay completely safe, you'd vacation at Disney World.) That said, there are rafting excursions for all skill levels, including children and seniors.

Rafting is a popular sport around the world, and there are numerous opportunities throughout the United States. East Coast locations include the Gauley River in West Virginia, the Kennebec River in Maine, and the Delaware River in New York and Pennsylvania. Western locations include the Grand Canyon, the Rogue River in Oregon, and the Salt River in Arizona. Excursions are also available in many states in between.

Why should you go? Because rafting is much more than simply racing down a river. It also provides an opportunity to observe nature, spend time with family, and make new friends. Rafters must work as a team, so relationships develop quickly.

FUN FACT

Rapids are divided into six classes based on difficulty. Class I is the easiest, and Class VI is the most difficult.

❑ 406. Walk the Dog with a yo-yo.

No, we're not talking about a pooch. We're talking about an object that can be released and pulled on a string. "Walk the Dog" is a favorite technique among people who are skilled with the yo-yo.

> **FUN FACT**
>
> In 1968, activist Abbie Hoffman was cited for contempt of Congress for, among other acts, "walking the dog" during a session of the House Subcommittee on Un-American Activities.

❑ 407. Play paintball.

Many of us older folks played Cops and Robbers when we were growing up. If we're honest, there's still a kid inside who wants to shout, "I got you!" How else to explain the 12 million people in more than 100 countries who are addicted to paintball? A variant on another childhood game called Capture the Flag, paintball involves shooting members of the opposing team with gelatin capsules filled with paint. Sounds silly? Of course it is. It's also tremendous fun. Again, 12 million players can't be wrong!

To get in on the action, look for a commercial paintball park. Most larger communities have one. Such parks are designed to ensure the safety of players by making certain everyone has the right equipment and knows how to use it. Resist the urge to buy paintball equipment and play in the woods in back of your house. That might seem like fun, but the majority of paintball-related injuries occur at such so-called "renegade" fields. Generally speaking, paintball is quite safe. As long as you follow normal safety precautions, you're unlikely to suffer anything more painful than a twisted ankle from tripping over an eliminated teammate.

Paintball Lingo

Like all sports, paintball has developed its own jargon. Here are a few phrases to get you started:

baller—short for "paintballer"

bounce—a paintball that hits you but doesn't break

B.Y.O.P.—"bring your own paint"

cyclops—a shot on your goggles, which looks like a single eye

dome shot—a hit to the top of your head

hoser—a paintballer who shoots too much paint

lit up—being shot so many times it's embarrassing

overshoot—shooting an opposing player more times than needed to eliminate them

soger—an aggressive paintballer

❑ 408. *Perform the Flying Dutchman from one jack to ten jacks.*

In this challenging variation of Jacks, you must toss the ball in the air, pick up a jack (or jacks) with the same hand, and then catch the ball with the same hand *without* letting it bounce. You must then place the picked-up jacks into the other hand while the ball is tossed in the air and then catch the ball after one bounce. Begin with one jack, and then do it again adding another jack. Continue to do it until you accomplish it with ten jacks. If you fail, you must start again with one jack.

You can purchase a set of jacks with a small rubber ball from most toy shops. Good luck!

❏ 409. Enter a poker tournament.

If you know when to hold 'em and know when to fold 'em, try your luck by entering a poker tournament. Poker, particularly Texas Hold 'em, has become a true spectator sport in recent years, with high-stakes tournaments regularly broadcast on television. An entire culture has sprung up around the game, with more and more people anteing up in hopes of winning a big pot.

Tournaments are easy to find, especially in Las Vegas and Reno, Nevada, and their East Coast equivalent, Atlantic City, New Jersey. Some require a sizable amount of money to enter, but tournaments with lower buy-ins are also available. Check the Internet, or consult your hotel regarding tournaments during your stay.

❏ 410. Attend the Indianapolis 500.

The Indianapolis 500 is perhaps the most famous automobile race in the country, if not the world. It attracts tens of thousands of spectators each year—and you should be one of those spectators at least once.

The 500 is held at the Indianapolis Motor Speedway, aka the Brickyard, and consists of 200 laps around a 2.5-mile track. Sure, you could stay home and watch it on television, but you haven't really lived until you've experienced the Indianapolis 500 in person.

Only three drivers have won the Indianapolis 500 four times each: A. J. Foyt (1961, 1964, 1967, 1977); Al Unser (1970, 1971, 1978, 1987); and Rick Mears (1979, 1984, 1988, 1991). And

A Bit of Indy History

The first Indianapolis 500 took place in 1911. American Ray Harroun won that race. The race has been run every year since, with the exception of 1917–18 and 1942–45, due to America's involvement in World War I and World War II.

lest you think the 500 is a men-only event, five women have competed over the years: Janet Guthrie (1977–79), Lyn St. James (1992–97, 2000), Sarah Fisher (2000–04, 2007–09), Danica Patrick (2005–08), and Milka Duno (2007–09).

To learn more about the Indianapolis 500, or to buy tickets, visit www.indy500.com.

☐ 411. Drive a Formula One car.

How would you like the opportunity to drive a high-performance race car at top speed and never worry about getting a ticket? It used to be that racing Formula One cars was just for the pros, but no longer. Now everyone with a driver's license has the opportunity to get behind the wheel.

The United States Formula One Driving Experience in Las Vegas offers everything you need to fulfill this high-octane fantasy. Students receive detailed instruction from experienced drivers, are taught the nuances of driving high-performance race cars (after all, this isn't the family jalopy you're maneuvering here), then let loose to drive just as fast as they want to. It's an exhilarating experience, but it doesn't come cheap. The basic course, which includes instruction and four laps around the track, will set you back almost $4,000.

So why should you do it? Because this may be your only opportunity to get behind the wheel of an authentic Formula One car, the undisputed king of racing vehicles. Two restrictions, however, are: You can't be taller than 6-foot-4, and you must know how to use a stick shift. For additional information visit www.racingschools.com.

■ ■ ■ ■

"Speed provides the one genuinely modern pleasure."

—Aldous Huxley

■ ■ ■ ■

❑ *412. Rent a Corvette for the weekend.*

It's everyone's dream to drive a fancy sports car. Unfortunately, if you're like most people, you probably can't afford it. But all is not lost. Instead of laying out big bucks to buy an exotic car,

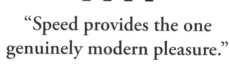

FUN FACT

In 1953, General Motors introduced the Chevrolet Corvette.

simply rent one for the weekend. Sure, it'll cost you more than the typical car rental, but think of the fun you'll have! Do it to celebrate a special occasion, such as your birthday or anniversary.

To find out who rents Corvettes and other sports cars in your area, visit ExoticCarRentalDirectory.com.

❑ 413. Learn to drive a stick shift.

Your friend has a new sports car and offers to let you drive it. It's shiny, it's beautiful, it's fast, it's...a stick shift. Bummer! You don't know how to drive a stick shift. It's been one of those mechanical things you're sure is too complicated to master. Maybe you've even tried once or twice to no avail. Don't give up! You can do this. A patient teacher, a can-do mindset, and a vacant parking lot are all you need to lick this nemesis. You'll feel like you've slain the dragon once you're behind the wheel of that sports car. Zoom!

Five Reasons to Drive a Stick Shift

1. Manual transmissions get better gas mileage.
2. In an emergency, you'll be able to drive a stick if necessary.
3. Clutches are less expensive to replace than entire transmissions.
4. You have better control in the snow and inclement weather.
5. Stick shifts are just plain fun to drive!

❑ 414. Drive cross-country.

Road trip! Does that stir up adventure in your soul, or what? Well, maybe it does, and maybe it doesn't...or doesn't yet, that is. Is there a place you've always wanted to go? Out East? Out West? Somewhere in between? Maybe you were thinking of flying there, but wait! What a great opportunity for a cross-country drive!

One of the wonderful things about road trips is that you'll forever remember the process of "getting there." The journey becomes a part of your destination. And if you don't have time to drive both ways, you can always fly one direction (to or from) and rent a car to drive the other.

If you're a camper, make some or all of your stops along the way camping stops. If you're more of a hotel comfort creature, it's never been easier than now to do online research and book the kind of rooms you prefer. If you're a member of AAA, you can even get their assistance planning your trip, including up-to-date maps and other helpful information.

And if you're brave enough to take some roads less traveled along the way, you'll be sure to find some unexpected beauty, novelty, and even some adventure. Consider the possibilities of hitting the road. It's a wonderful way to get there, wherever "there" may be.

A Few Famous Cross-Country Routes

Route 66 (California to Chicago). Alias, "The Mother Road" or "Main Street of America," this cross-country route is still the most popular highway for tourists.

US-50 (California to Maryland). This is the last non-interstate transcontinental highway left in the United States, wandering 3,200 miles coast-to-coast.

US-80 (California to Georgia). This 3,000-mile stretch of roadway runs across the warm southern states.

❑ 415. Adopt a stretch of highway through the "Adopt-a-Highway" program.

Have you ever driven down a road and wished you could stop, get out of your car, and pick up the litter that has accumulated? Well, there's a way you can do just that.

> ### Call Your State DOT
>
> Not all states have the Adopt-a-Highway program, but you can contact your state department of transportation to find out if your state participates or if it is planning to do so in the future. Participating states include Arizona, California, Connecticut, Delaware, Kansas, Maryland, Massachusetts, Nevada, New Hampshire, New Jersey, New York, Pennsylvania, Rhode Island, Utah, and Washington state.

The Adopt-a-Highway program is an anti-litter, roadside-cleanup campaign many states have employed to promote statewide pride and ownership in keeping roadways looking clean, free of traffic hazards, and environmentally healthy. The program not only helps keep the state clean, but it also helps taxpayers save money and reminds people not to litter. Businesses, clubs, organizations, schools, religious groups, civic groups, and even families can participate in this great American cleanup effort.

❑ 416. Travel the Pacific Coast Highway.

California is famous (and infamous) for its traffic congestion. But that shouldn't prevent you from taking a drive along the Pacific Coast Highway, one of the most scenic stretches of road in the country.

The Pacific Coast Highway, also known as State Route 1, passes through several towns and cities, including Santa Monica, Monterey, San Francisco, and Los Angeles, and offers much to admire along the way. Of particular interest to the scenically inclined are those portions that directly follow the

> **Driving Caution**
>
> If you're going to travel the Pacific Coast Highway, it's best to do it during the off-season. The route courses through several very popular beach resorts, and traffic can be bumper to bumper during the summer months.

coast. Other sights of interest along the drive include the Golden Gate Bridge and Los Angeles International Airport (LAX). In fact, a portion of the highway extends directly beneath two LAX runways.

Construction on what is now the Pacific Coast Highway began in 1919, and repair proceeds to this day, because earthquakes and other natural phenomena continue to damage it, requiring routine maintenance. It's a highway unique among highways and should be traveled at least once in your lifetime. Preferably in a convertible in nice weather.

❑ *417. Tour wineries in Napa Valley.*

Many states produce fine wine, but California is perhaps the best known, thanks in great part to Napa Valley. And for good reason: The region is home to more than 300 wineries, many of which offer tours and tastings.

Located north of San Francisco, Napa Valley has been producing wine since 1861, when Charles Krug established the area's first commercial winery. Great soil and excellent weather made for good grapes, and within three decades more than 140 wineries were in operation throughout the region. Sadly, a surplus of grapes, followed by the arrival of a destructive root louse called phylloxera, almost destroyed the industry before it could take off.

Today, tourism is almost as big as wine-making in Napa Valley, and several companies offer excursions to area wineries, where you can watch wine being made and sample the product. Most tours hit several different wineries, so you can taste (and purchase) an eclectic variety of vino. The region also hosts numerous festivals and other events throughout the year.

☐ *418. Attend a wine tasting.*

Does your wine knowledge consists of "white with fish, red with beef"? Are you overwhelmed by the number of choices in the wine aisle? Try attending a wine tasting to expand your wine horizons. A knowledgeable instructor can explain the different types of wine, tell you how to serve them, and help you find wines that you'll really enjoy. The best wine tastings are at vineyards, of course, but if the climate in

How Sweet It Is?

What's the difference between sweet and dry wines? It's all about fermentation, as yeast digests sugar—either naturally occurring from the grapes or added by the vintner—and produces alcohol. The more fermentation, the less sugar remains and the drier the wine.

your area doesn't support winegrowing, better restaurants and food merchants often sponsor wine tastings as well. Bring along a notepad so you can jot down the names of wines you like.

☐ 419. Enjoy an excellent wine.

Make a good meal even better by complementing it with an exceptional wine. Don't purchase just any wine; good wines are expensive, but they are worth it. Visit a wine shop, and don't hesitate to ask the proprietor for advice.

☐ 420. Make your own wine.

Jesus made a name for himself by turning water into wine at a wedding in Cana. You can impress your friends by making wine, too. It won't make you divine, but it will probably get you invited to more parties.

Home wine-making has really taken off in recent years, and several companies sell wine-making kits that include all the equipment and ingredients you'll need to ferment several gallons of vino. (You can find them at many wine specialty shops.) This approach is probably better, and safer, than trying to wing it using instructions cobbled off the Internet.

Although grapes are the most popular and best-known ingredient for making wine, you can make homebrew out of almost any kind of fruit, including apples, peaches, raspberries, and pears. Start off with a basic grape wine, then once you've got the hang of it, take it to the next level with whatever fruit strikes your fancy.

The key to making good wine is not to rush the process. Proper fermentation takes time, so leave your jugs alone. When your first batch is ready, invite your friends over for a tasting.

❏ 421. Create your own unique beverage.

Everyone should create something truly original before they die. One fun option is to invent a signature alcoholic beverage.

Don't worry, you don't need an advanced degree in mixology. Start with a drink that you already enjoy, such as a screwdriver or a martini, and spice it up with something special, such as an unusual fruit juice or a dash of another alcoholic spirit. If you're feeling really adventurous, simply mix and match various ingredients until you find just the right combination. Finally, give your blend a creative name—one that'll sound sophisticated when someone calls for another at your next party.

❏ 422. Make your own beer.

Not a wine drinker? Never fear—you can also make your own beer!

Homebrewing has been a popular hobby for decades, and complete kits are available in most states. You'll find them in a variety of places, including hobby shops, larger liquor stores, and wine specialty shops. Making your own brewski is a fun hobby, and once you get the hang of it, it will cost less than buying commercial beer.

Homebrewed beer can be just as delicious as the store-bought stuff. And you don't have to worry about being stuck making just one kind of beer; kits are available for creating a wide variety of suds. Like wine, homebrewed beer takes time and patience. In fact, you're looking at several weeks from step one to pouring your first chilled one. According to homebrew afficionados, it's well worth the wait. There's a special satisfaction that comes with doing it yourself.

It's important to note that some municipalities have laws concerning homebrewing, so make sure you check with authorities before proceeding. For more information on homebrewing, consult the American Homebrewers Association at www.beertown.org.

■ ■ ■ ■

**"Beer is proof that God loves us
and wants us to be happy."**

—Benjamin Franklin

■ ■ ■ ■

❑ 423. Visit Hersheypark in Hershey, Pennsylvania.

"The Sweetest Place on Earth" is a 121-acre amusement park situated in Hershey, Pennsylvania, near the Hershey Chocolate Factory. With more than 60 rides and attractions, including 11 roller coasters and 11 water rides, the park offers plenty of pure fun for the entire family. A wave pool, as well as various entertainment venues and dining options, round out the attractions.

Hersheypark is more than 100 years old. It first opened on April 24, 1907, as a leisure park for the employees of the Hershey Chocolate Company and was later opened to the public.

Chocolate Kisses

Hershey produces more than 80 million Hershey's Kisses every day at its factories in Pennsylvania and Virginia. How the candy got its name has been lost to history, though one theory suggests that it was named after the sound or motion of the chocolate being deposited during the manufacturing process.

❏ 424. Drink and/or sing in an Irish Pub.

In Ireland, pubs (short for "public houses") are more than just places to drink. They're also community centers where people eat, meet friends, listen to music, and are encouraged to chime in with voice or instrument. Everyone's Irish in an Irish pub.

■ ■ ■ ■

"Few things are more pleasant than a village graced with a good church, a good priest and a good pub."

—John Hillaby

■ ■ ■ ■

❑ 425. Attend a Shakespeare play in the outdoor theater in Ashland, Oregon.

Calling all theater lovers! Each year from February to October, the Oregon Shakespeare Festival (OSF) repertory actors take the stage (or stages, rather—there are three of them). The Tony Award–winning festival, founded in 1935, is one of the nation's oldest and largest professional non-profit theaters.

Of the 11 productions each season, four or five are from the works of Shakespeare. The remaining plays include both classic and contemporary selections. The three stages on the campus include the outdoor Elizabethan Stage (or Allen Pavilion), which is a replica of Shakespeare's Globe Theatre, the New Theatre, and the Angus Bowmer Theatre.

The town of Ashland is an experience in itself, with people, buildings, and landscape portraying early 17th-century England. And, if nothing else, you must see a Shakespeare play at the Elizabethan Stage to bring you back to merry old England.

❑ 426. Take a magical mystery tour.

Do you feel as though the walls are closing in on you? Expand your horizons by taking a magical mystery tour! Ride a bus or commuter train to the end of the line and explore the neighborhood. Most likely this is a part of town you've never visited before. Check out the shops. Have lunch in a restaurant or diner. Chat with the people you meet. How is this neighborhood different from yours? How is it the same?

It's a big world out there, with a lot to offer those who are willing to look beyond their own limited confines. Explore and enjoy.

❏ 427. Drive a Zamboni.

Everyone knows that the true hero of the skating rink is the guy who drives the Zamboni. The next time you're at your local skating palace, quietly slip the guy $20 and see if he'll let you take it for a spin.

■ ■ ■ ■

"There are three things in life that people like to stare at: a flowing stream, a crackling fire, and a Zamboni clearing the ice."

—Charlie Brown

■ ■ ■ ■

❏ 428. Complete a century bicycle ride.

If the last bicycle you rode had training wheels, it's time to bike without them and start practicing for a century bike ride. That's not how long you ride, it's how far—100 miles. Challenging? You bet! But think of how good you'll feel when you finish that 100th mile.

There are three types of century rides:

■ A self-planned, unsupported century in which you pick the route and set your own schedule. Pros: You're not dependent on anyone and can ride at your own pace. Cons: You may face unexpected obstacles along your route and will need to carry your own tools and supplies in case of emergency.

■A brevet, which is a pre-planned ride in which you pay a small fee for a map of a route that usually includes information on supply stops along the way. Brevets come in a variety of distances, with the shortest option usually being 125 miles.

■An organized century, in which your fee covers food and mechanical assistance along a safe, established route. Local bike clubs sponsor most organized centuries.

A century ride requires a certain degree of physical fitness and should not be attempted by anyone who is out of shape or in ill health.

Century Tips

Endurance is the key to a successful century. If it's been a while since you've ridden a bicycle, practice for a few months to build stamina and become familiar with your bike. Touring bikes come in different weights and styles, so consult a local bike shop to see which is best for you.

❑ 429. Go horseback riding in the mountains.

Imagine yourself... shades of *Man from Snowy River*: You're on a sturdy horse, heading up a mountain path, the further up you go, the better the vistas become. Soon you're "on top of the world," looking out over the tops of 60-foot-tall trees, and the mountain air…Ahh!

Here are some basic horseback riding tips:

- Keep your legs under you, not swinging too far forward or backward.
- Keep your feet parallel to the horse's sides. (Don't stick your toes out.)
- Keep your heels down and your arms, wrists, and fingers relaxed.
- Don't ride alone. Have an instructor or experienced rider nearby.

❑ 430. Ride a horse on the beach.

We've all seen those ads featuring people riding horses on the beach. Trust us—this is something you should definitely do.

■ ■ ■ ■

> **"There is something about the outside of a horse that is good for the inside of a man."**
> —Winston Churchill

■ ■ ■ ■

❑ 431. Take a horse-drawn carriage ride.

Sometimes the best way to see a new city is not by bus or car but by horse-drawn carriage! This is especially true when you're accompanied by someone you love.

The horse-drawn carriages that take riders around New York's Central Park are some of the most famous in the world, but they're not the nation's only carriage rides. Many other municipalities also offer carriage excursions, including Chicago, Illinois; Charleston, South Carolina; and Philadelphia, Pennsylvannia.

If at all possible, take your ride in the spring or fall, when the weather is neither too hot nor too cold. And don't forget to tip your driver.

■ ■ ■ ■

"The wind of heaven is that which blows between a horse's ears."
—Arabian Proverb

■ ■ ■ ■

□ *432. See North Carolina's wild horses.*

FUN FACT

The wild horses on Shackleford Banks are commonly known as "Shackleford ponies" because of their small stature.

North Carolina is renowned for many things, including excellent barbecue and a passion for college sports. Unknown to many, however, are the wild horses that have lived for generations on the state's Outer Banks. Make plans to see them while you still can.

The federally protected horses that frolic on Shackleford Banks, Ocracoke Island, and elsewhere in North Carolina are believed to be descended from Spanish stock that arrived in the region more than 400 years ago. To see them run wild and free is a remarkable sight to behold and a memory that you'll carry with you forever.

❑ 433. Ride an elephant.

It's the dream of every child to ride an elephant, so if the opportunity ever presents itself, go for it. You'll feel like a 12-year-old again!

Many American zoos and amusement parks offer elephant rides, as do various locations around the world, including several African nations, Bali, and Thailand, where elephants are commonly used as beasts of burden.

FUN FACT

Elephants can live 70 years or more. They generally reach puberty around age 14, and females bear young until they are about 50 years old.

Warning: Don't expect a smooth ride. Sitting atop an elephant can be a bit rocky, so make sure you hold on tight!

❑ 434. Wash an elephant at the Elephant Nature Park in Thailand.

Not many people can say they've bathed an elephant. Your chance awaits at the Elephant Nature Park in Chiang Mai Province in northern Thailand. The park is a conservancy for rescued elephants, where visitors are encouraged not just to look at but also to physically interact with the playful pachyderms. You can feed them fruit from a viewing platform and bathe them in the river that runs through the compound.

In Thailand, the logging industry often uses elephants for hauling timber. The Elephant Nature Park takes in those that have been injured or are too old to continue working. It also has an active elephant breeding program.

■ ■ ■ ■

"I have a memory like an elephant. In fact, elephants often consult me."

—Noel Coward

■ ■ ■ ■

❑ 435. Ride a camel.

Camel rides aren't as common in the United States as elephant rides, though opportunities do exist. Your chances of making this dream come true, however, are greater if you visit the Middle East. Egypt, in particular, has made camel rides an essential part of the tourist experience.

Riding a camel can be challenging because they tend to be moody animals, and they're not exactly built for comfort. That said, if a camel has a saddle and you've got the time, you should definitely hop aboard. After all, you may never get another chance.

■ ■ ■ ■

"I distrust camels, and anyone else who can go a week without a drink."

—comedian Joe E. Lewis

■ ■ ■ ■

❑ 436. Swim with dolphins.

Anyone who watched *Flipper* on television as a child or who has visited a major aquarium knows how much fun dolphins can be. Watching them frolic is one thing—actually being in the water with them is a dream come true.

Attractions that offer the opportunity to swim with dolphins have popped up throughout the world, including the Bahamas, Jamaica, Mexico, Australia, and Africa. Not surprisingly, the United States has its share, including several in Florida. In fact, there are so many that one could make a week's vacation out of traveling from the Florida Keys north to Tallahassee, visiting one dolphin attraction after another.

Most attractions offer the opportunity to physically interact with dolphins by swimming with them, riding them, and encouraging them to perform tricks. Many also offer packages that include photos and a DVD of your time with the playful sea mammals. Visit the Internet or check with your travel agent for attractions near you that feature dolphin-swim opportunities.

A Cautionary Note About Dolphins

Be wary of attractions that advertise encounters with wild dolphins. This may sound like fun, but untrained dolphins can be unpredictable and even dangerous. Keep in mind, too, that it's against federal law to harass or feed wild dolphins.

❑ 437. Go whale watching.

The largest mammals on earth are not elephants....They're whales! Whales use oxygen via lungs, not gills, giving them mammal status.

In 1950, whale watching emerged as an organized activity in San Diego when the Cabrillo National Monument was declared a public location for viewing gray whales. Since then, whale watching has grown into a significant part

of the tourist industry worldwide. In 1998, one study concluded that 87 countries have whale-watching operations.

From the deck of a whale-watching vessel, you may be fortunate enough to view whales breaching (jumping out of the water) or tail slapping (smacking tails against the surface of the water). Depending on what region of the world and what time of year you choose to whale watch, you may be able to see not only whales but also dolphins or porpoises. Some of the types of whales that can be glimpsed include blue (the earth's largest mammal), gray, sperm, humpback, fin, minke, right, and orca. And though you may choose to participate in a private whale-watching expedition with friends, you can also hook up with any one of a number of good commercial whale-watching tours. The advantage of a commercial tour includes experienced guides and knowledgeable staff, who can maximize your experience with instructive information and by providing your best chance of (safely) viewing the whales.

❑ 438. Go shark diving.

Anyone who has seen the movie *Jaws* knows that sharks are not to be messed with. That said, there's nothing quite like the adrenaline rush of diving among these sleek, toothy predators. Every year, a growing number of thrill-seekers travel the world just for the opportunity to slip into a dive cage and interact with sharks in their natural habitat. Several companies offer shark-diving excursions—and promise the experience of a lifetime.

The types of sharks you'll see depend on where in the world you drop your cage. Not surprisingly, the most popular shark dives involve Great White sharks, the massive eating machines made famous in Peter Benchley's best-selling novel. Shark dives, however, can also put you in close proximity to 30-foot whale sharks, tiger sharks, bull sharks, thresher sharks, and many others.

You usually don't have to be an experienced diver to participate in a shark dive. Since you're primarily just spending time in a cage under water, most companies will train and prepare you, in addition to videotaping this exceptional, once-in-a-lifetime experience as a special souvenir.

■ ■ ■ ■

"Sharks are as tough as those football fans who take their shirts off during games in Chicago in January, only more intelligent."
—Dave Barry

■ ■ ■ ■

❏ *439. See polar bears in their natural environment.*

If you're really intrigued with polar bears, you should put them at the top of your must-see list because global warming is rapidly eating away at their natural habitat. Unless conditions change, these noble beasts may become extinct in our lifetime.

Polar bears live in the Arctic region, but they can also be found in Canada, Greenland, Norway, Russia, and the United States. They're the largest predators in their environment, and they typically dine on seals. They depend on rapidly diminishing sea ice for their survival, which is why global warming has become such an important issue.

Many international tour companies offer excursions to the polar bear's natural environment, where these majestic creatures can be seen and photographed going about their daily lives. Such tours have become increasingly popular in recent years as the environmental danger to polar bears increases.

Polar Bears Thrive in the Cold

Polar bears have adapted well to the extreme conditions of their arctic environment, where winter temperatures can plunge to -22 degrees F. A thick layer of fat insulates them from the cold, and their coat is comprised of water-repellent fur that conserves heat, allowing them to swim in frigid water without harm. In addition, their skin is black, which helps them absorb heat from the sun.

❑ 440. See penguins in their natural habitat.

Penguins are proof that God has a sense of humor. (They're also proof that everyone looks good in a tuxedo.) If you've seen penguins only in a zoo or aquarium, take the plunge and see them in their natural habitat.

Many people believe that penguins live only on the frozen plains of Antarctica, but that's not true. There are 17 different species of penguins, and they are spread throughout the Southern Hemisphere, from Australia to South America to South Africa. In fact, one of the world's most accessible penguin colonies is located just a few miles from Capetown.

Some penguin colonies are located on islands so remote that they're reachable only

> ## A Giant Among Penguins
>
> The Emperor penguin is the largest of these remarkable flightless birds, often reaching four feet in height and weighing as much as 90 pounds. They live in Antarctica, an inhospitable ice desert where the temperature can plunge to -140 degrees F.

by research vessel. Luckily, there are many other opportunities to view penguins in the wild, and numerous tour companies offer excursions specifically for people who find penguins so much fun. Depending on where you'll be traveling next, check the Internet or consult your travel agent for available penguin adventures.

❏ 441. Visit the San Diego Zoo.

If your idea of the perfect vacation is seeing the world's most magnificent animals up close and personal, pack your bags for the internationally acclaimed San Diego Zoo. Established in 1916, the park boasts more than 4,500 mammals, birds, reptiles, and amphibians, in addition to a botanical garden with plants and trees from around the world.

Every dollar raised through the sale of tickets, food, and souvenirs goes back to support the work of the Zoological Society of San Diego, which is dedicated to the conservation of endangered species and their habitats. Its work extends far beyond California, supporting research and preservation efforts throughout the world.

When you go to the San Diego Zoo, plan to spend the entire day. Exhibits and attractions include Tiger River, an Asian rainforest bioclime; Ituri Forest, where you will see the elusive okapi, swamp monkeys, and river hippos; Gorilla Tropics, home to a variety of primates; Reptile Mesa; Giant Pandas; and Polar Bear Plunge. Be sure to also see the San Diego Wild Animal Park in the San Pasqual Valley outside the city of San Diego. The Zoological Society of San Diego also runs this park.

The Wegeforth Vision

The San Diego Zoo was the brainchild of Dr. Harry Wegeforth. It began with a small group of animals left over from the 1915–16 Panama–California International Exposition in Balboa Park. One day Wegeforth heard the roar of the Exposition's lions and decided on the spot to establish San Diego's first animal park.

❑ 442. Visit the Bronx Zoo.

The Bronx Zoo is one of the most famous zoos in the United States, as well as one of the oldest. It opened to the public in 1899. No trip to New York would be complete without a side visit to this remarkable menagerie. Though located in the middle of a major metropolitan city, the

Bronx Zoo boasts an eclectic array of exciting exhibits, including African Plains, Congo Gorilla Forest, Jungle World, Tiger Mountain, and Madagascar! Indoor exhibits include Bug Carousel, Mouse House, World of Darkness, World of Reptiles, and World of Birds.

The Bronx Zoo is open year round. For tour information, visit www.bronxzoo.com.

"I love acting, but it's much more fun taking the kids to the zoo."

—Nicole Kidman

❏ 443. Volunteer at a big cat reserve.

If your love of cats includes the big kind, such as lions and tigers, help their cause by volunteering at a big cat reserve. Dozens of big cat sanctuaries can be found across the United States. Most are nonprofit facilities that take in animals that have been abandoned by private owners, circuses, and zoos. It takes a lot to care for them, so your time and assistance will be greatly appreciated. Just make sure you don't come to work smelling of bacon.

❏ 444. Visit an alligator farm.

Alligator farms are a great way to see these scaly behemoths up close without losing a limb. If you've never visited one before, you're in for a wild experience.

Florida is home to several alligator parks, including the Everglades Alligator Farm in Homestead and the St. Augustine Alligator Farm. Louisiana also has several commercial alligator farms, including Bayou Pierre Alligator Park outside of Natchitoches and Insta-Gator Ranch & Hatchery in Covington.

In addition to live alligators in their natural environment, most parks also sell gator-related products ranging from canned meat to leather boots. Good to know if you're shopping for a unique holiday gift.

■ ■ ■ ■

"Never insult an alligator until after you have crossed the river."

—Cordell Hull

■ ■ ■ ■

❏ *445. Go birdwatching.*

Birdwatching can be a great way to relax and commune with nature. And best of all, it's free. Every region of the United States has its own unique species of birds, but many species also migrate, which requires brief visits to places they are not normally seen. Spotting and identifying these feathered vacationers can be challenging and fun.

Regional birdwatching clubs and societies are common throughout the United States, and

> ### Birdwatching Tips
> Birdwatching is commonly done in natural habitats, but if natural locations are unavailable, you can lure birds to your own backyard by providing frequent food, water, and opportunities for nesting.

they will be happy to give you pointers regarding the best birding locations and what to look for. You'll need some basic equipment, including an illustrated bird guide (available at most book stores), binoculars, a pen and paper to record your findings, snacks and water, comfortable boots or sneakers, and a waterproof pouch to carry your stuff. You may also want to bring a camera to photograph the birds you see.

Birding is a great family activity and a wonderful way to get kids outside for some fresh air. It's also educational. For tips and other information, visit www.birdingguide.com.

❑ 446. Watch the swallows return to San Juan Capistrano.

Every October, thousands of cliff swallows leave Mission San Juan Capistrano in San Juan, California, for their winter migration to Argentina. And every March, almost always on or around the 19th, they return. For decades, the swallows' amazing feat has been cause for a huge celebration.

According to legend, the swallows took refuge at the mission after an angry shopkeeper destroyed their mud nests. They are now officially protected by town ordinance, which makes it a crime to damage their abodes.

❑ 447. Build an ant farm.

Ants are nature's most industrious critters. Watch these six-legged dynamos at work by building your own ant farm!

If you had an ant farm as a kid, you know how entertaining they can be. You can buy an ant farm kit at a toy store, or you can build your own ant farm by carefully transferring an ant colony from your back yard to a clean gallon jar. (Use a rubber band to cover the top with gauze so the ants can breathe.) Feed your tiny pets small pieces of fresh fruit, and add a few drops of water every few days. With care, your ants should thrive for several months.

> ### Ant Life
> Ant mounds typically consist of several chambers connected by tunnels. The chambers are used for nurseries, food storage, and as resting places for worker ants. Army ants are unique in that they don't build a permanent home; instead, they travel in large groups searching for food.

❑ 448. Hold a butterfly in your hand.

Nature is beautiful and begs to be admired. The next time the opportunity arises, gently hold a butterfly in the palm of your hand and marvel at its design. Then let it go and watch it fly away until you can no longer see it.

Wild butterflies are plentiful in the spring and summer and are attracted by colorful flowers. If you live where butterflies are uncommon, take a trip

> ### FUN FACT
> With a wingspan of 11 inches, the Queen Alexandra's birdwing, found on the island of New Guinea, is the world's largest butterfly.

to a local butterfly center, where these gorgeous critters can be found in abundance. For a list of the best butterfly centers in the United States, visit www.americasbestonline. net/index.php/pages/butterflycenters.html.

❏ 449. Train squirrels to take peanuts from your hand.

Want to really impress your family, friends, and the folks next door? Teach the neighborhood squirrels to take peanuts from your hand. The key is patience. Squirrels tend to be skittish yet inquisitive, so sit quietly in an area where squirrels congregate and place peanuts all around you. As the squirrels become accustomed to your presence, bring the peanuts closer and closer to you. Finally, sit motionless with a peanut in your hand until a squirrel finally retrieves it. Once the squirrels realize that you have food and mean them no harm, they'll come running up to you every time you step outside. But be careful so as not to get bitten.

"Even a blind squirrel finds an acorn sometimes."

—proverb

❏ 450. Foster a homeless dog or cat.

Tens of thousands of wonderful dogs and cats are sitting in shelters just waiting for someone to adopt them. Lend a hand by offering to foster one or two until a good home can be found for them.

A growing number of animal shelters around the country have started foster programs to help ease overcrowding. Every animal sent to a foster home is one fewer than might have to be euthanized. In most cases, the shelter provides veterinary care and assists with food and other necessities.

❑ 451. Adopt a pet from a shelter.

Is there room in your home and in your heart for a new furry friend? Consider adopting a cat or dog from your local animal shelter. The benefit of a shelter adoption is that it's a win-win situation for pet and person alike. For the pet, it means a new home with a loving owner rather than "institutional living" or being "put to sleep." For the person it means being able to choose a pet that suits his or her personality and situation.

To help you find the right critter, the shelter can usually provide a profile and history for each animal. If the pet you're considering has any endearing qualities or problem behaviors, you can know these in advance and make an informed decision. Another perk is that animals are adopted

---

Top Five Reasons to Adopt a Pet at a Shelter

You'll Save a Life. In the U.S., 3–4 million homeless cats and dogs are euthanized annually.

You'll Get a Healthy Pet. Most shelters examine and vaccinate animals.

You'll Save Money. Adopting is less expensive than buying pets.

You Won't Be Supporting Puppy Mills via Pet Stores.

You'll Feel Better. Pets are psychologically, emotionally, and physically beneficial to you.

---

at a minimal cost, which usually includes spaying/neutering, updated shots, worming, and in some cases, a microchip ID service. Some shelters will even throw in some extras, such as a new collar or a bag of pet food. You can do research online or over the phone as far as costs and what is included, but it's that trip to the shelter that will end up captivating your heart.

❑ 452. Teach your pet a special trick.

The person who said you can't teach an old dog new tricks obviously never had a dog. Bond with your dog, cat, or other favorite animal, and entertain your friends at the same time, by teaching your pet a special stunt.

Professional animal trainers know that the best way to teach an animal a trick is to make the process fun. This means proceeding slowly and rewarding your pet with a tasty treat every time it does what you want it to. Practice for a brief period several times per day, and your pet should be performing like a pro within a week.

> ### Reward, Not Punish
> Teaching an animal to perform a trick should never involve punishment. And remember, some animals learn faster than others. Be patient, reward success, and encourage your pet to perform its new trick until it becomes effortless.

❑ 453. Attend a serious dog or cat show.

Perhaps you've seen a dog or cat show on television. To truly experience this subculture, however, go to one of these shows in person. They are everywhere. The action of these competitions is actually fun, but even better is to visit the areas where the dogs or cats are prepped, primped, and primed.

□ 454. *Tour an aircraft carrier.*

Aircraft carriers have long been the unstoppable juggernauts of modern warfare. Tour one of these amazing floating cities to see what's been helping keep America and its allies safe for generations.

Several retired aircraft carriers are docked around the country, and almost all of them offer tours to the public. Among the most impressive are:

- The USS *Hornet,* Alameda, California. Daily tours are available, and four times per year, visitors can spend the night. Visit: www.uss-hornet.org.

- The USS *Yorktown,* Charleston, South Carolina. The centerpiece of Patriots Point Naval and Maritime Museum. Visit: www.patriotspoint.org.

- The USS *Midway,* San Diego, California. Conveniently located alongside Navy Pier on the Embarcadero. Visit: www.midway.org.

- The USS *Lexington,* Corpus Christi, Texas. One of the most famous and heroic aircraft carriers in all of U.S. naval history. Visit: www.usslexington.com.

Most retired aircraft carriers are floating museums that chronicle the ships' history-making sailors and missions. Many saw significant action in World War II. Don't worry if a trip to a retired aircraft carrier isn't physically practical for you. Active carriers occasionally dock in large port cities and are available for tours by civilians. Watch the news for the next visit in an area you may be able to access.

❏ 455. *Visit a historic battlefield near your home.*

Many epic battles have been fought on American soil over the past 300 years. If you haven't visited a designated site in your state, you're missing a remarkable piece of history. An eclectic array of historic battlefields and military parks dot the United States, and chances are good that there's at least one close to your hometown. The National Park Service maintains most of these sites and offers guided tours. You'll also find displays of relics and personal accounts from their specific battles.

❏ 456. *Visit the Tomb of the Unknowns at Arlington National Cemetery.*

The military has continuously guarded this tomb since July 2, 1937. Buried there, representing unidentified American soldiers who have died in battle, are three unidentified servicemen: one each from World War I, World War II, and the Korean Conflict.

During the hours that the cemetery is open to the public, the guard is changed (during summer months) every half-hour in a ten-minute ceremony of careful precision and reverent honor. On the tomb you'll read the moving epitaph:

> "HERE RESTS IN HONORED GLORY
> AN AMERICAN SOLDIER KNOWN
> BUT TO GOD."

❑ 457. Record a WWII veteran's memories of his/her experiences.

World War II was a time of bravery and tragedy, of great loss and of great national unity. Although the men and women who experienced that time are passing away, it's not too late to record their memories for future generations. Today's digital recording technologies make it easy to capture those memories and preserve them. Most computers let you plug in a small microphone (many have them built-in), and free software that's available online lets you edit and even add music to your recordings. Before you begin, make a list of questions you'd like to ask, but be open to sidetracks—sometimes the most interesting stories won't be the ones you think to ask about.

❑ 458. Visit the USS Arizona Memorial.

Japan's attack on Pearl Harbor on December 7, 1941, was, to quote President Franklin Roosevelt, "a day that will live in infamy." The more than 2,300 American servicemen and civilians who perished in the attack are honored at the USS *Arizona* Memorial.

A total of 1,177 crewmen lost their lives aboard the *Arizona,* which is considered "ground zero" in the Japanese assault. The 184-foot-long memorial structure spanning the mid-portion of the sunken battleship consists of three sections: the entry and assembly room; a central area designed for ceremonies and general observation; and the shrine room, where the names of those killed on the *Arizona* are engraved on a marble wall. The guided tour of the USS *Arizona* Memorial includes a 23-minute documentary film depicting the attack on Pearl Harbor, a short boat trip, and a self-guided exploration of the memorial. Tickets to the memorial are free and distributed on a first-come, first-serve basis. Keep in mind that the wait to go to the memorial can be lengthy, especially during the summer months.

❑ *459. Visit the WWII Memorial in Washington, D.C.*

It is a moving experience to stand in the very center of history when that history has not fully passed from our memories. You probably know someone who was alive during World War II, but before they are all gone take time to visit the WWII Memorial in Washington, D.C. It's worth a trip to our nation's capital if you haven't yet seen this relatively new monument. You can stand before this memorial and feel the contributions of those who participated in this most pivotal time of the 20th century.

■ ■ ■ ■

**"This generation of Americans
has a rendezvous with destiny."**

—Franklin Delano Roosevelt

■ ■ ■ ■

460. Visit the American Cemetery and Memorial in Colleville-sur-Mer, Normandy, France.

Whether or not you know someone who served in the European theater of World War II, you can't help but be moved by the sight of 9,387 graves of American soldiers killed in the D-Day offensive, the prelude to the end of the war in Europe some 11 months later. Included are four women, one father-and-son pair, and 33 sets of brothers. The names of another 1,557 soldiers who are missing and their bodies never recovered are also inscribed in the memorial.

From this cemetery, one can see out over the beaches on which so many of the deaths occurred. British, Canadian, and American forces landed on the Normandy beaches—Utah, Omaha, Gold, Juno, and Sword—in the largest amphibious assault in history. This now peaceful and orderly site sits at the same location as the temporary graveyard that was quickly assembled while the battles still raged, on June 8, 1944. That temporary site was the first American cemetery established on European soil in that war. The cemetery is open to the public with guides on hand to escort families to specific gravesites upon request.

461. Visit a Nazi concentration camp.

The barbarous treatment of those interred in Nazi concentration camps during World War II remains an indelible stain on our collective soul. Ensure that the world never forgets this dark moment in human history by visiting one of these camps or reading a book by a concentration camp survivor.

Several Nazi death camps in Poland remain open for tours, including Auschwitz, Treblinka, and Majdenek. And one of the most powerful books by a concentration camp survivor is *Night* by Elie Wiesel, a young Orthodox Jew who was sent to Auschwitz and Buchenwald with his family. It's a harrowing story and one that everyone should read.

❏ *462. Participate in the Bataan Memorial Death March.*

Every year, the Army ROTC Department at New Mexico State University, White Sands Missile Range, and the New Mexico National Guard sponsor the Bataan Memorial Death March to honor the brave soldiers who endured the actual Bataan Death March during World War II. The memorial march, held at White Sands Missile Range in New

> ## Casualties of the March
> Tens of thousands of American and Filipino soldiers were involved in the Bataan Death March in April 1942. Thousands died during the 60-mile forced march, and those who survived endured tremendous hardship as prisoners of war.

Mexico, has grown from 100 to about 4,000 participants annually. They come from across the United States and around the world. Many march in honor of a family member or a particular veteran who was in the Bataan Death March or who was taken prisoner by the Japanese in the Philippines.

The Bataan Memorial Death March features two routes. The longest—and most grueling—is a 26.2-mile hike that takes you across hilly desert terrain. A 15-mile route is also available. Be advised that the Bataan Memorial Death March is a strenuous event and should not be attempted by anyone who is not in good physical condition.

❑ 463. Visit the Korean War Veterans Memorial.

If everything you know about the Korean Conflict is based on reruns of *M*A*S*H,* do yourself a favor and visit the Korean War Veterans Memorial in Washington, D.C. This moving tribute to the American men and women who fought Chinese and North Korean aggression from 1950 to 1953 includes 19 lifelike statues sculpted by Frank Gaylord (14 Army, 3 Marines, 1 Navy, 1 Air Force); juniper bushes meant to symbolize the rough terrain service members encountered in Korea; and a Mural Wall consisting of 41 panels extending 164 feet and containing 2,400 unique images.

❑ 464. Visit the Vietnam Memorial in Washington, D.C.

In its polished black surface you can see your own reflection as you read the names chiseled into its face. Names that represent lives—lives of soldiers who never returned from the uncertain and sultry days and nights they spent fighting against communism in Southeast Asia. Seeing your own face peer back at you from the surface of those somber black slabs reminds you that you are there, alive, free. And you are there, looking at the price of freedom—the lives, represented by the names.

■ ■ ■ ■

"The soldier, above all other people, prays for peace, for he must suffer and bear the deepest wounds and scars of war."

—Douglas MacArthur

■ ■ ■ ■

❑ 465. Thank a war veteran for his/her service to our country.

Don't ever be afraid to express your heartfelt thanks for a military man's or woman's willingness to put his or her life on the line for our country. The purpose of these soldiers was and is a worthy one: to protect and preserve the freedom of all Americans.

Veterans Day: A Day to Honor Military Veterans

On November 11, 1918, the signing of the Armistice, which ended World War I, became the designated day to honor military veterans in the United States. This would later become known in America as Veterans Day—a day to show honor, respect, and gratitude to the men and women who have served in wartime and peacetime.

❑ 466. Plant a tree in someone's memory.

Finding meaningful ways to remember a loved one is comforting, and planting a tree is a wonderful way to commemorate that person's life. Spend time finding the right tree. Then select a special spot and let the planting be a ceremony of remembrance.

■ ■ ■ ■

"What does he plant who plants a tree?
He plants the friend of sun and sky."

—Henry C. Bunner, *The Heart of the Tree*

■ ■ ■ ■

❑ 467. Buy food for a homeless person.

No matter how bad things are, they could always be worse. Pay forward your good fortune by buying food and drink for the next homeless person you see standing on a corner and holding a sign. And let your generosity come from your heart.

■ ■ ■ ■

"No kind action ever
stops with itself. One kind
action leads to another."

—Amelia Earhart

■ ■ ■ ■

❑ 468. Volunteer at a homeless shelter (and not just during the holidays).

Each year at holiday time you may get the notion to call your local homeless shelter or soup kitchen and volunteer your time. *Resist this urge.* Turns out that lots of good people have the same idea as you do every year. Many of these organizations report getting overwhelmed with volunteers at holiday time but find themselves short-handed come March or April. So at holiday time, look at next year's calendar, pick a date in the "off-season" that works for you, and call the shelter or agency right then to ask how and when you can best help.

■ ■ ■ ■

"The life of a man consists not in seeing visions and in dreaming dreams, but in active charity and in willing service."

—Henry Wadsworth Longfellow

■ ■ ■ ■

❑ 469. Help sponsor an Olympic athlete.

It takes a lot of skill to win an Olympic medal. A lot of money, too, because training isn't cheap. Guide an athlete along the path to victory by helping to pick up part or all of his or her bill. Why? Because the United States government does not fully finance the training of its Olympic athletes the way other countries do. And depending on the sport, training can cost tens of thousands of dollars per year, a fact that keeps many promising athletes out of the running.

There are a lot of ways to assist Olympic athletes, but the easiest is to become a personal sponsor. This is something best pursued by wealthy individuals, but the rewards can be many. If you're not independently wealthy, perhaps you could form a group to "invest" in an athlete. If you own a large business, you can also become a corporate sponsor. This is how many professional athletes in nonsalaried sports have their training underwritten. An endorsement deal of this nature is a win-win for both your business and the athlete you're sponsoring.

❏ 470. Volunteer for your local Special Olympics.

Looking for a great way to give back to your community? Volunteer with your local Special Olympics, in which everyone is a winner!

In 1962, Eunice Kennedy Shriver started a program that would become the Special Olympics. It was a summer day camp for children and adults with disabilities. It proved so popular that, in 1968, the first International Special Olympics Summer Games were held at Soldier Field in Chicago. One thousand men and women with disabilities from 26 states and Canada competed in track and field and swimming. Today, the Special Olympics hosts athletes with disabilities from more than 180 nations.

The Special Olympics holds regional competitions, and volunteers are always needed for various jobs, including registering athletes, planning events, arranging transportation, and publicizing activities. In addition, those looking for on-the-field action can become involved by joining Special Olympics Unified Sports, in which people with and without disabilities train and compete together on the same team.

To learn more about the Special Olympics and to find out about volunteer opportunities in your region, visit www.specialolympics.org.

■ ■ ■ ■

"Let me win, but if I cannot win, let me be brave in the attempt."

—Special Olympics motto

■ ■ ■ ■

❑ *471. Volunteer your time with a cause that uses your special talents.*

If life has been good to you, pay it forward by volunteering your time with a cause that can use your special talents.

Everyone is good at something that can benefit others. For example:

- If you have a pleasant voice, offer to read newspapers and magazines to the vision-impaired.
- If you're good with animals, help out at a no-kill shelter.
- If you're a skilled cook, volunteer at a local women's shelter.

❑ 472. Contribute to a cause you believe in but haven't actively supported.

Do you give to your favorite charities on a regular basis? If so, good for you! But this year, carry it forward by contributing to a cause you believe in but haven't actively supported in the past. Everyone has issues that are important to her or him. For example, if you like animals, write a check to your local no-kill shelter. Other possibilities include environmental organizations, groups that assist the homeless, and those that protect our civil liberties. Whatever your beliefs, take a moment to support those that are doing good work. Your donation doesn't have to be a lot; every dollar helps.

■ ■ ■ ■

"True charity is the desire to be useful to others without thought of recompense."

—Emanuel Swedenborg

■ ■ ■ ■

❑ 473. Make an anonymous donation.

It's nice to be recognized for our accomplishments, but not all good deeds need to be done in public. The next time the opportunity arises, make an anonymous donation to a worthy cause. And enjoy the satisfaction that comes with performing an unselfish act.

❑ 474. Host a fundraiser for a charitable cause.

It's said that charity begins at home, so do your part for a benevolent cause close to your heart by hosting a private fundraiser. Your life will truly be enriched.

■ ■ ■ ■

"He who wishes to secure the good of others, has already secured his own."

—Confucius

■ ■ ■ ■

❑ 475. Donate your hair to charity.

If your hair is longer than 10 inches, help a child in need by donating it to Locks of Love! This nonprofit organization turns donated ponytails into high-quality hairpieces for financially disadvantaged children who suffer from long-term medical hair loss. Many of the recipients are victims of a condition called alopecia areata, for which there is no known cure. Others have experienced hair loss from radiation therapy and chemotherapy, severe burns or trauma, and various other genetic and dermatological conditions.

Locks of Love is in constant need of long ponytails from which hairpieces can be created. Many hair salons are affiliated with the organization and are more than happy to help you wash and cut your hair, and then send it to the organization's offices in West Palm Beach, Florida. And you don't need to turn to a hair salon to make a donation; you can trim and ship your hair yourself if you wish.

The hairpieces provided by Locks of Love go a long way toward restoring the self-esteem and confidence of children victimized by hair loss. So if your hair is just hanging around, put it to good use. For information on how to donate, visit www.locksoflove.org.

❑ 476. Donate blood.

Whether you're type A, B, AB, or O, what's pumping through your veins right now is the liquid of life! If you're able to, give blood regularly at a local blood bank. It's the gift of life. And it's as simple as that.

❑ 477. Become a bone marrow donor.

If you regularly donate blood, consider taking the next step and become a bone marrow donor. Your kindness could help save someone with leukemia, lymphoma, or other life-threatening diseases.

Organizations such as The National Marrow Donor Program (www.marrow.org) and the American Bone Marrow Donor Registry (www.abmdr.org), as well as hospitals with marrow transplant programs, are in constant need of marrow donors. Participants must be a genetic match, and registries help connect donors with appropriate recipients.

Potential marrow donors must be between the ages of 18 and 60 and in good health. If you are selected as a possible match for a patient, you may be asked to donate bone marrow or cells from circulating blood, known as a PBSC donation. If that match is good, you will be scheduled for an actual marrow donation. Your donation can literally mean the difference between life and death for someone in need.

Keep in Mind

Donating bone marrow is more time-consuming than donating blood. Moreover, unlike donating blood, some bone marrow programs charge a fee for donor participation. This is to offset the high cost of maintaining the registry and type-matching your marrow in the hope of finding an appropriate recipient.

❑ 478. Become an organ donor.

Give the gift that keeps on giving—become an organ donor. It's easy, and it's free. The next time you get your driver's license renewed, make sure it lists you as an organ donor, and carry an organ donor card in your wallet at all times. In addition, make your family aware of your decision; their permission may be required to harvest your organs at the time of your death.

Becoming an organ donor is a remarkably generous act. The need for donated organs far exceeds the number that become available each year, so your decision may ultimately save or improve the lives of many people.

When people think of organ donation, they usually think it's only the heart or the kidneys. Many organs, however, can be harvested and transplanted into others in need, including the corneas, lungs, intestines, liver, and pancreas. You're never too old to donate your organs, and in many cases, even those with chronic illnesses can still donate when they pass away.

Organ donation is a big decision, but it's a great way to help people in need. For more information on how to become an organ donor and what the process entails, visit www.organdonor.gov.

❑ 479. *Participate in the Breast Cancer 3-Day fundraiser walk.*

Has breast cancer ever touched you in some way? If so, what is your story? Are you a survivor of this disease? Have you lost a friend or loved one to it? Does it run in your family? The Breast Cancer 3-Day is a way to add a positive chapter to your story. This 60-mile walk is the journey toward a cure for a disease that impacts both men and women. (And speaking of men, they can and do participate as well.)

If you are not able to walk, you might consider participating as a volunteer or a crew member. Volunteers commit to helping with some element of the event, while crew members are those who are available to help for four days with the entire event.

❑ 480. *Leave an outrageous tip for an overworked waitress or waiter.*

Waiting tables is hard work. Toss in the factors of temperamental customers, difficult coworkers, cooks who may get orders wrong, and a demanding supervisor, and you've got a recipe for virtual insanity. Yet they arrive at your table with a smile, asking to take your order.

❑ 481. Visit three people in a nursing home or hospital.

Thousands of people live in a nursing home, and many of them have no one to come visit them. You can change that. Make plans with friends to visit at least three people in a nursing home or hospital. (The staff can give you recommendations and make introductions.) Ask leading questions that encourage your hosts to talk about themselves, and always be interested, polite, and cheery.

Your visit will make the day a little brighter for the people you meet, and you may come away with a handful of new and fascinating friends.

❑ 482. Volunteer at a nursing home.

During the holidays, nursing homes bustle with visitors. For some residents, however, weeks can stretch into months between holidays before another visitor comes to see them. As a volunteer, you can play an important role in the lives of people who would relish the opportunity to spend some one-on-one time with you. Conversation is something many residents long for and enjoy most. Playing games, taking walks, hearing retrospective stories, and singing are a few other favorites.

Nursing home staffs are often stretched to the limit with just taking care of the residents' most basic needs. As a volunteer, you can bring that extra TLC to make someone's day.

❏ 483. *Gather friends and sing at a retirement center.*

Nursing homes and retirement centers can be lonely places to live, especially if you don't have family to visit you anymore. Brighten a lot of spirits by gathering some friends to sing at a local facility—and do it on a non-holiday, when residents don't get as many visitors.

It doesn't matter if you don't sing like Streisand or Sinatra. What's important is that you've taken the time to bring a little joy to a group of people who don't have as much in their lives anymore. So sing loudly and from the heart, and watch the smiles spread.

❏ 484. *Host a foreign exchange student.*

Would you like to help bolster international relations? Then show an inquisitive teenager how wonderful the United States can be by hosting a foreign exchange student. As a foreign exchange host, it will be your responsibility to make sure that your exchange student has a fun, educational experience abroad. This means ensuring that the student's school experience goes well and that he or she has an opportunity to see all that the United States has to offer through immersion in American culture.

Most foreign exchange students speak fairly good English, and their stay is relatively brief—typically just a few months—so your obligation is not extensive. You don't have to have children of your own to be a foreign exchange host, though having youngsters of the same age around can certainly make an exchange student feel more comfortable.

❏ 485. Teach someone to read.

The United States is one of the most powerful nations in the world, and yet a frightening percentage of its population is illiterate. In 2000, it was estimated that 42 million Americans were unable to read and 50 million were unable to read above a fifth-grade level. Help fix this problem by teaching someone to read.

What You Can Do

Literacy programs can be found in every state and almost every large city. Volunteers receive training and then are paired with individuals in need of reading assistance. Participation requires a relatively small amount of your time, and yet it can have a dramatic impact on someone's life. Imagine people's joy when they read a story to their children for the first time—all because you offered to help.

❏ 486. Mentor a child.

It doesn't take much time to make a difference in a child's life. A mentor who faithfully shows up to weekly appointments brings a level of camaraderie and predictability into a young person's life that may not be there at home.

Check with your local school district or your community youth center to find out if it has a mentoring program. After an application process and background check, you'll be given rules and parameters to help keep you and the mentoree safe from potential issues or problems. From there, you'll embark on a fun, sometimes challenging, but definitely rewarding relationship with someone who could use a grown-up friend.

❏ 487. Put together a jigsaw puzzle with a child.

Simple pleasures are often the most enjoyable. One such pleasure is putting together a jigsaw puzzle with a child. Use that time to share your wisdom, and maybe learn a little something in return. Children can surprise you if you give them the chance.

❏ 488. Assemble the most difficult jigsaw puzzle you can find.

Brace yourself. The most difficult puzzle has 24,000 pieces, and it's about 14×5 feet! It's aptly titled "Life—the Great Challenge," created by Royce B. McClure. Okay, so maybe it's something to work up to . . . and save up for, as it retails for $380. Meanwhile, find the hardest and most intriguing jigsaw puzzle at your local toy store.

❏ 489. Sponsor a child in a developing country.

There's considerable poverty in the world, and children are its most innocent victims. Help make our world a much better place by sponsoring a child in a developing country. Contributing to the welfare of a child in need is a generous act and is easier and less expensive than you might think. There are numerous organizations in place to help, and most ask for a contribution that equals less than a dollar per day. That's less than most people spend on a cup of coffee.

Most international relief organizations directly connect you with a specific child. Your donations typically go into a communal fund that assists the entire village, but the child with whom you're paired is a real person who will share his or her life and experiences with you through letters and photographs.

The monies donated to international child sponsorship efforts go toward a variety of worthy goals, including more nutritious food, the building of schools, vaccinations against deadly diseases, and clean water. It's amazing how so little money can help so many.

❑ 490. *Help end world hunger by supporting ONE.*

We live in an era of abundance, and yet people all over the world die of starvation every day. More than 500 million people in Asian, African, and Latin American countries are living in "absolute poverty." It doesn't have to be that way, however, and you can help by becoming a supporter of ONE.

ONE (www.one.org) is an international grassroots campaign and advocacy organization backed by more than two million people who are committed to bringing an end to poverty, hunger, and other problems, especially in Africa. ONE attempts change through active support. It places a spotlight on the world's most pressing problems and on those who have offered a public commitment to addressing these problems. It also holds accountable those who are responsible, while campaigning for better development policies, more effective aid, and trade reform. Furthermore, the program supports greater transparency to ensure that policies to end poverty are implemented effectively.

❑ 491. Build a house with Habitat for Humanity.

Handy with a hammer? Do something nice for your community by volunteering to assist your local Habitat for Humanity. Established in 1976 by Millard and Linda Fuller, Habitat for Humanity International has built and rehabilitated more than 300,000 homes around the world. The organization has affiliates in almost every major American city and is in constant need of volunteers. That's where you come in.

> ### Financing for Habitat Homes
>
> Habitat for Humanity is not a giveaway program. The houses it builds are sold to partner families at no profit and financed with affordable loans. The homeowners' monthly mortgage payments are used to build more Habitat houses.

Each affiliate coordinates all aspects of Habitat home building, including fundraising, building site selection, partner family selection and support, house construction, and mortgage servicing. Local affiliates are asked to support international Habitat efforts by donating 10 percent of the money they raise. This program raises millions of dollars to address poverty throughout the world.

You don't have to be a skilled builder to assist Habitat for Humanity. People of all levels of skill and experience are welcome, and construction professionals who are on site will be more than happy to show you what to do. If you are unable to perform physical labor, you can help by donating money or materials. There's a special satisfaction that comes from helping the underprivileged, and Habitat for Humanity provides the perfect opportunity to do just that.

❑ 492. Serve in the Peace Corps.

Since 1961, thousands of Americans have served their country and the world by joining the Peace Corps. They assist in such areas as education, the environment, student outreach, and information technology. If you have 27 months to donate, visit www.peacecorps.gov.

❑ 493. Participate in a nonviolent protest.

There's a lot of good in the world but, sadly, a lot of bad as well. Show your righteous anger by participating in an organized, nonviolent protest for something you strongly believe in. Peaceful protest is one of the cornerstones of our democracy and one of the most effective ways to give voice to important issues and enact change. When enough people make a point, those in charge are forced to listen.

The key tenet, of course, is nonviolence. Nonviolent protest brings important issues to light.

❑ 494. Adopt an endangered species.

Are you in need of a unique gift for that special someone? Why not symbolically adopt an endangered species in his or her name through the World Wildlife Fund (WWF)? The WWF offers a variety of adoption packages, from which more than 80 species are available to adopt. For a $50 dona-tion, your special someone will receive a soft plush version of the adopted animal, a Species Spotlight card containing fascinating facts about the animal, a 5″×7″ adoption certifi-cate suitable for framing, a 5″×7″ color photo of the adop-tion animal, and a drawstring gift bag.

For further information on how to symbolically adopt an endangered species, visit www.worldwildlife.org.

❏ 495. Break a bad habit.

No one's perfect. Almost all of us have flaws that need cor-recting, whether it's a bad habit or something worse. Now's the time to figure out what needs fixing in your life and take care of it. For most people, that flaw is little more than a bad habit, such as biting their fingernails or cracking their knuckles. All of these are somewhat easy to fix if you put your mind to it.

If your problem is something more serious, such as an addiction to tobacco, alcohol, or drugs, you should enlist the assistance of a professional. There are several free cessa-tion programs for smokers, and Alcoholics Anonymous or a similar program can help if addiction is keeping you from your full potential.

Tips for Breaking a Bad Habit
To kick a bad habit, you also have to tackle the complementary behaviors around it. For example, if you find yourself constantly eating unhealthful snacks while watching television, cut down on your television viewing and substitute something more nutritious, such as veggies, for those times when you do snack.

❑ 496. Ask for forgiveness from someone you've hurt.

Increase goodwill in the world by asking for forgiveness from someone you've hurt. Make the request in person or by phone (not e-mail), and be sincere in your apology. Promise to be more thoughtful in the future.

■ ■ ■ ■

"There is no love without forgiveness, and there is no forgiveness without love."

—Bryant H. McGill

■ ■ ■ ■

❑ 497. Forgive someone who has wronged you.

Holding a grudge is never a good use of your time, because the only person it hurts is you. Instead, sincerely forgive the person who wronged you. Whether you let that person know is up to you; what's important is how you feel in your heart.

❑ 498. Turn an enemy into a friend.

What? An enemy to a friend? It may seem unthinkable at first. Of course, this feat of the heart and mind requires specific action. All of the mental and emotional gymnastics we go through to try to convince ourselves that we have forgiven someone are pretty much a waste of time without any corresponding action. This being the case, show kindness, gentleness, humility, patience, compassion, concern, consideration, and plain old-fashioned love. It may take some time. It may not be easy. But in the end, it will be well worth it. Meanwhile, little by little (or perhaps all at once) the iceberg of your enemy's disdain for you might just melt into the refreshing gift of friendship.

❑ *499. Be kind to a stranger.*

Kindness to strangers costs nothing, and the rewards are many. So be the first to offer a smile, give up your seat on the bus or train, or buy a cup of coffee for the person behind you. Maybe they'll pay it forward.

■ ■ ■ ■

"I have this theory that if one person can go out of their way to show compassion then it will start a chain reaction of the same."

—Rachel Scott (first victim of the Columbine High School shootings)

■ ■ ■ ■

❑ *500. Give a surprise gift to that special person in your life.*

No. It doesn't count if the gift is a birthday present or if that gift is for any other special occasion. Your gift must be spontaneous—out of the blue—and simply because you love that person so very much.